To
BRAD,

Best wishes and
always "Stand Tall"

STAND TALL

Stand Tall

Dr. Isaiah "Ike" McKinnon

~

Foreword by Jennifer Granholm, Michigan Attorney General

Sleeping Bear Press

Sleeping Bear Press
310 North Main Street
P.O. Box 20
Chelsea, MI 48118
www.sleepingbearpress.com

Printed and bound in Canada.

10 9 8 7 6 5 4 3 2 1

Library of Congress Cataloging-in-Publication Data

McKinnon, Isaiah.
  Stand tall / by Isaiah "Ike" McKinnon with Barry Gottlieb ;
foreword by Jennifer Granholm.
       p. cm.
ISBN 1-886947-96-1
1. McKinnon, Isaiah. 2. Police—Michigan—Detroit—Biography.
3. Afro-American police—Michigan—Detroit—Biography.
4. Police chiefs—Michigan—Detroit—Biography. I. Gottlieb,
Barry. II. Title.
HV7911.M363 A3 2000
363.2'092—dc21

00-010414

Preface

At the beginning of most of my speeches, I emphasize the fact that I have had a wonderful life. Should I die tomorrow, let it be known that I would have few regrets. This child from a family of limited means, but vast dreams, is, in reality, living out the American Dream.

When I joined the Detroit Police Department in 1965, I would occasionally jot down a note or key word to later refresh my memory about significant events that have occurred over the years. And when I retired as Chief of Police of the City of Detroit in 1998, little did I realize how these notes would play such a pivotal part in the writing of this book.

This is my personal memoir. It is a history of some of the major events that I have either taken part in or have observed in my life. It is a story of pain. It is a story of brutality, and it is a story of racism. It is these things that begin my story, but they don't end it. More importantly, it is a story of reconciliation, of commitment, of dedication, of love, of guidance, of fortitude, of hard work, of sacrifice, and of service to family, community, and country.

Mine is a story of a Detroit boy, mentored, guided, educated, and loved by many. It is also the story of the people who helped make me who I am. This book is a tribute to them.

Their efforts have not been in vain.

Foreword

You cannot choose your battlefield,

The gods do that for you,

But you can plant a standard

Where a standard never flew.

NATHALIA CRANE, *THE COLORS*

I believe in fate. I believe in the idea that we are each part of a bigger, more important whole and that there are, in this world, forces greater and stronger than all of us. I believe that in the end, some things are just meant to happen and that some things—like Vernor's ginger ale and vanilla ice cream, or Ernie Harwell and Tigers baseball—are just meant to be together. Ike McKinnon and the City of Detroit are exactly those kinds of things.

From almost the moment that Ike and his city found each other nearly 50 years ago, they have been the perfect reflection of each other's courage and determination to succeed. Together, they have reveled in each other's victories and found strength in the face of each other's challenges.

For as long as I have known him, Ike McKinnon had sung—literally— this city's praises and celebrated her people. Though he could have gone anywhere and chosen any path in life, Ike chose to make a lifetime out of serving the people of Detroit. Or maybe Detroit chose Ike—either way, we're all the better for it.

Jennifer M. Granholm
Michigan Attorney General

Acknowledgments

I thank first of all my wife and partner Patrice, the love of my life, for her beautiful smile, for being my guide through a wonderful life together, and for the birth of our two sons, Jeffrey Christopher and Jason Patrick. Without their love, support, and encouragement, this book might have remained just an idea.

To my parents, Cota and Lula McKinnon, who gave me life, a foundation to build on and a will to succeed, and to be forgiving.

To my sons Jeffrey and Jason, God blessed not only your mother and me with you, but also the world. If only my parents were alive to see how proud we are of you both and how their legacy continues in you.

To my grandparents by marriage, Peter and Magdalena Holzschuh, two people whom I only had the pleasure of knowing for a brief period of my life, but their bold, youthful journey from Yugoslavia, patriotism for America, and commitment to fairness will forever be a part of my life.

To my sisters, Gloria, Ada, Helen, and Bernice, and brother Cota. And to my brothers-in-law, Charles and the late Reverend James Jones. Also to my many nephews, especially Brian Keith, Cody, Mark, Edward, and Justin Isaiah.

To the Sciarini family, especially Uncle Jim and Aunt Mac, and my favorite cousins, Jim, Judi, Mike, Sue, and Denise. With special memories to Primo and Rose Sciarini.

To the Hiller and Vogel extended families.

To Mayor Dennis W. Archer for his vision of the city of Detroit, for the paths we traveled together and for selecting me as his Police Chief.

To Michigan Attorney General Jennifer Granholm, thank you for your support of my family and me.

To Senator Carl Levin, now they will believe that you, Ron Thayer, and I actually played basketball together.

To Cardinal Adam Maida, who is not only a great religious leader, but also a bridge builder who continues to do the best for all, especially the young.

To Sister Maureen Faye and the University of Detroit Mercy family, especially the Department of Education and Human Service.

To Father Norman Thomas and the Sacred Heart Catholic Church family.

To Professor Angela DeWitt, clinical psychologist, for her scholarly advice on the finalization of this book.

Many thanks to all of my Detroit Public School teachers for my educational foundation, specifically Lincoln Elementary, Garfield Junior High, and Cass Technical High.

To my two Irish-American brothers Bill and Neal Shine and their families for the profound impact you have all had on my life, and the quality of life for my family.

To Will and Tina O'Sullivan, Pete and Pat Kinnahan and their families for your lasting friendship and our wonderful family memories.

To my beautiful goddaughter Jennifer O'Sullivan, you make us all so proud.

To my godmother Cathy Wagner, we will be forever blessed to have you in our lives.

To Kathy Dekovich for being my wife's lifelong friend, and to her husband Dr. Alex Dekovich for his friendship and thought-provoking conversations.

To Marge and Terry Kasparian, our Pennsylvania connection. It's time to come home.

To Tom, Carol, and Johanna Katroscik and the Stoop Ball League of America, founded in Clinton, Wisconsin.

To Michael and Nancy Timmis, two of the most caring, giving, and thoughtful people I have had the pleasure of knowing.

To Steve Horn, the former CEO of the Renaissance Center, a friend and great tutor about the ways of the business world.

To former Mayors Jerome P. Cavanagh and Judge Roman Gribbs, for the example you set not only as politicians, but as men.

To Curtis Blessing, my friend and former neighbor, thanks for opening the door.

To my friend and attorney Justin C. Ravitz, a visionary who still maintains a quest for equal justice for all.

To Joe Dumars, for the examples you have set, not only as an athlete and businessperson, but as a husband, father, and friend to many.

To Bob Webber, since high school, what a life of friendship and smiles, and actually being bold enough to ask me to sing at his wedding.

To Frank and Elaine Mitchell, thank you and your family for being colorblind.

To Greg "Smo" Smolinski and Jose Hardrick and my office staff for your friendship and the countless hours of your time protecting my family and me.

To Dave Simmons for your advice, friendship, and guidance.

To Mr. Raymond G. Hughes, Mr. Bunche, and all of my nosy, caring neighbors, who all made a difference in my life and in the lives of so many others.

To Danny Steinke, my Windsor, Ontario leukemia survivor who is an inspiration to us all.

To Dick Purtan and Tom Ryan from Oldies 104.3; to Mitch Albom and Paul W. Smith from WJR; to Linda Lee, Bob Schuman, and Kevin O'Neill from WYCD; to Alexander Zonjic from Smooth Jazz and John Mason from Mason in the Morning, for allowing me to share my views and experiences with you and your audiences.

To Mark "Doc" Andrews for your guidance, support, and friendship.

To Mort Crim, a friend and advisor whose voice and "Second Thoughts" are heard and cherished by so many.

A special thanks to Alan Frank and Deborah Collura of WDIV-TV in Detroit for your insight, and the opportunity you gave me.

Many thanks to special friends in the media:

Carmen Harlan, Emery King, Bob Bennett, Huel Perkins, Al Allen, Cheryl Chodin, Devin Scillian, Ruth Spencer, Dave Grant, Jack Kresnak, Jim Titsworth, Kevin Deitz, Mike Lewis, Chuck Gaidica, Diana Lewis, Val Clark, Bernie Smilovitz, Diana Kozar, Paula Tutman, Roger Weber, Paul Gross, Reynolds Wolfe, Karen Drew, Marcella Lee, Michael Ann Wolf, Bill Proctor, Ann Thompson, and the wonderful Lila Lazarus.

To Sleeping Bear Press, Adam Rifenberick, and many others for this exceptional opportunity.

A sincere thank-you to the men and women of the Detroit Police Department who have touched my life in so many ways, especially to the families of Officers Jerry Philpot, Lindora Smith, Patrick Prohm, and Sergeant Earl White, officers who lost their lives in the line of duty during my tenure as Chief of Police. My heart will always be heavy because of their sacrifices.

To all of my military friends, especially Josia Bell, Haron Rayls, Dick, and, of course, Ellis "Combat" Brown, God bless you all for the wealth of memories.

And in loving memory of my cousin Larry Ross, whose name is one of the many on the Vietnam Memorial Wall.

To my family, past, present, and future, for what you have done, what you are doing, and the legacy you will leave.

The wolf shall live with the lamb,

the leopard shall lie down with the kid,

the calf and the lion and the fatling together,

and a little child shall lead them.

ISAIAH 11:6

INTRODUCTION

Newly elected Mayor Dennis Archer walked up to me in the hallway of the Bates Academy and said, "Well homey, are you ready?" I smiled and said, "Let's do it." We shook hands and hugged. The smiles on our faces spoke volumes. I walked up the stairs, accompanied by my wife Patrice and our sons, Jeffrey and Jason. There were people lining the hallways, filling the doorways, and spilling out into the corridors as we made our way to the auditorium. As we entered, I was blinded by flashbulbs and lights from the TV cameras. We made our way through a sea of schoolchildren and dignitaries. It seemed as though every one of them were reaching out to shake the mayor's hand. I looked around and saw the heads of virtually every law enforcement agency in Southeast Michigan—the FBI, the Michigan State Police, the Sheriff's Department, and the prosecutor's office. It was a blur—an exciting, head-spinning blur, and a wonderful, magical moment.

The mayor spoke to the assembled students—I can't say that I remember much of it—and then introduced my wife and my sons. I smiled proudly when I heard him say, "I introduce to you the next chief of police of the city of Detroit, Dr. Isaiah McKinnon."

The applause was deafening. I kissed Patrice, and then reached for my oldest, Jeffrey, and then Jason. My emotions were running wild as I stepped up to the podium. Time stood still. They say that your life flashes before you as you're dying. I don't know about that, but it certainly did at that moment in my life. I remembered the things that had made an impact on my life, and the people who said and did things that propelled me toward this moment, both good and bad. I fought back a tear as I thought about the two most important people of my life—my parents, Cota and Lula McKinnon—who weren't there to be a part of this. For a brief moment, I stared out into the sea of people and flashbulbs and said to myself, "They're looking down now and smiling because their son is the new chief of police." I thought about Mr. Hughes and Mr. Bunche. I thought about Father Shea and Combat Brown in Vietnam. And I thought about Rotation Slim.

∼

It was a crisp, sunny September afternoon in 1957 when I left Garfield Junior High School, after visiting my former woodshop teacher and mentor, Mr. Raymond Hughes. I was thinking, "Life doesn't get much better than this." I had just started at Cass Technical High School, one of the best schools in the country. I was proud to have been selected to go there—it was really quite an honor, especially since I was one of the few blacks to be accepted. I had gone back to Garfield to tell Mr. Hughes about the incredible opportunity that I had been given and to thank him for everything he had done over the years.

As I left, I ran into a friend. He was an older guy from the neighborhood and one of the only fellows with a car. He offered me a ride home in his faded green Chevy, and as we pulled out of the parking lot a big black police cruiser flagged us down. Two officers jumped out—half of "the Big Four."

"The Big Four" was a group of white police officers that patrolled our neighborhood and got gratification from intimidating and hurting people. There was a group of young black men who hung out on the corner of St. Antoine and Superior talking, singing, and minding their own business, but every once in a while, for no apparent reason, "the Big Four" would pull up beside them and jump out of their car. They were very large and intimidating men who were always heavily armed. They'd throw the young black men against the car, or prone on the sidewalk, and search them for no apparent reason, with one officer aiming a machine gun or shotgun at them. They'd hassle the young men, tell them to get the hell off the corner, call them a bunch of derogatory names and drive off laughing.

I saw this and other similar scenes often, but when you're fourteen years old and don't hang out on the streetcorners or get in trouble, you don't envision anything like that ever happening to you. How wrong I was.

One of "the Big Four" who climbed out of the car that day was Rotation Slim. He was a tall, gangly man with dark hair who was notorious in the neighborhood. He'd scream at people on the street and smack them around for no reason. Word of mouth was that he'd killed a few black people, including a prostitute. I don't know whether this was true or not, but, because the perception existed at all, it was more effective than any truth could ever be. Here's what I knew: He had beaten others and there was never any recourse for the beaten. I was terrified of joining this fraternity of the defenseless many, but I was as powerless as they demanded I be.

He and his partner pulled my friend and me out of the car, searched us, stripped the seats and trunk, and were as abusive and nasty as they could be. Rotation Slim grabbed me and threw me against the car.

"Sir?" I was frightened, without a clue of what I had done wrong.

He hit me in the chest hard, slamming me into the car. I couldn't believe this was happening. I hadn't done a thing!

"Sir?" I asked again, starting to cry.

He hit me again. And again. He and his partner began to beat me, knocking me against the car. Out of the corner of my eye, I could see my friend getting beaten as well. At fourteen, I stood six-foot-one and weighed 170 pounds—and they beat me good. The more I asked why they were doing it, the more they hit me. And the harder I cried, the harder they slammed me into the car.

They were good at this. They knew not to hit me in the face where it would show. They pounded my chest and my stomach, and called me every vile, derogatory racial slur you can imagine. In the brief moments between blows, I felt as if the world had come to an end. I thought that they were going to kill me. I honestly did. These were the police—the law—and for no reason at all they were doing to me what I'd seen them do to the men on the corner. I was crying and looked around for help. People came out of their homes and watched, but there was nothing they could do. This was everyday life in the neighborhood.

When they finally had enough they told us "niggers" to get the hell out of there. They never asked who we were, what we were doing, or why we were there. They beat us because we were handy. And because we were black.

I ran the ten blocks home crying, confused, and in pain. I knew that I couldn't tell my parents, because if I did my mother would go down to the 13th Precinct and confront them, and that wasn't a good idea. In those days, if a black person went to the police to make a complaint, they were often arrested themselves. Or worse. If they'd beaten me for no reason, what would they do to my parents if they went in and complained?

For years, I didn't tell anyone about the incident. I kept it locked up inside me. It resided right next to the vow I made that night that one day I was going to join the Detroit police department, and that I would do everything in my power to make sure nothing like this ever happened to me again, or to anyone else. I sat in my room that night and promised myself that I was going to make a difference in peoples' lives.

∾

I beamed as I stood in front of the crowd at the Bates Academy, flanked on either side by my wife and two sons. When the mayor handed me that gold badge with the words "Chief of Police, City of Detroit" stamped on it, I was overcome with emotion. I looked down at the badge, then looked up at the children who filled the auditorium. They were children who had their whole lives ahead of them. They were lives that held the potential for greatness, for happiness. I flashed back to 1968.

~

I was three years out of the military, having spent time in the Strategic Air Command and in Vietnam. I was in great shape, at 6′2½″ and 222 pounds, and was proficient in the martial arts. I was a member of the Detroit police department and on patrol with my partner, a chunky white officer with red hair who, at the time, had a well-deserved reputation for poor personal hygiene. Being a young black officer on the predominantly white police force, I, like many of the other black recruits, was often assigned to partners with whom no one else necessarily wanted to work.

We stopped at Big Ben's, a restaurant on Woodward Avenue across from the Bonstelle Theater. When we walked inside, my partner let out a whistle. "Wow, it's Rotation Slim!"

"Who?" I asked, as the very mention of the name was making my blood boil.

"Rotation Slim," he repeated, pointing to a lanky, aging man sitting in a booth at the rear of the restaurant. "He's a legend in the department."

There he was, sitting right in front of my eyes. He was wearing a white shirt, a tie, and brown pants—not unlike any other off-duty police officer. But he was different. I saw myself backed up against the patrol car while this man and his friends beat me. I heard their taunts. I felt the pain. I knew their hatred.

"That's Rotation Slim?" I asked. My mind was clouded by every tear that I had cried that day in 1957 and in the weeks that followed.

I looked at the man, and felt my fists clench at my side. I wanted to rip his heart out. I wanted my pound of flesh. I stormed toward him, the fourteen-year-old boy now a man, ready to avenge the hurt, the pain, and the tears that I had kept bottled up inside.

I towered over him as he sat at his table. His hair, still black, now shrouded the weather-beaten face of a much older man. He just stared into space as he sat there by himself, sipping his coffee. Every sensibility that I had was heightened as I tried desperately to look him right in the eye, but he never made a move to look at me. "Rotation Slim?"

He looked up. "Yes, officer?"

After being filled with so much rage, I strangely felt it ebb away. This man, who once called me every derogatory name you can imagine, had just called me "officer."

I repeated his name. "Rotation Slim. Well, well, well." His coffee cup shook in his hand. "A number of years ago you did something to me that changed my life."

His eyes were wide. His hand shook more. His cup rattled against the saucer and produced a clanging noise that permeated the tense air between us. Drops of coffee splashed on the table. "What did I do?" he asked, his voice uneasy, cracking. "Tell me, what did I do?"

Looking down at this shrinking, shaking, pitiful man, I suddenly felt a weight lift from my shoulders. This cowardly excuse for a police officer had undoubtedly beaten many people—probably black and white alike—for no other reason than that was how he got his kicks. He didn't know who they were or what ever happened to them. And he didn't care. As long as he had his gun at his side—which he did at that moment—he felt that he would never be held accountable for his past. He hurt the helpless; he abused his power. Just seeing him in front of me shaking as I stood over him gave me the pound of flesh I needed without having to take it by force. I had my reconciliation.

"You won't remember what you did," I told him, thinking of the image I saw reflected in the mirror that morning—me standing proud in my clean, pressed police uniform. "You won't remember it at all. But you know something? I want to thank you for it."

I smiled and walked away.

≈

I thought of this as I stood at the Bates Academy holding that shiny chief's badge. I thought about the fourteen-year-old who had been brutally beaten by four cops for no reason. I thought about the naive police recruit who had struggled to maintain his dignity and morals in the face of racism and corruption. I thought about the one-time poster boy for the department. And now I was standing next to the new mayor of Detroit. All eyes were on me.

I smiled. And I swear to you I muttered to myself, "Thank you, Rotation Slim."

CHAPTER *one*

M‌y father, Cota McKinnon, was born in June of 1900 in Bullock County, Alabama. My mother, Lula Bell, was born there in 1909, although it wasn't until they'd each moved to Montgomery, Alabama that they met, got married, and had eight children. Ada was the oldest, and then came my brother Cota, Jr. I was born next, followed by Helen Marie, and Gloria Jean, the youngest. There were three others—George Edward, Elizabeth, and an unnamed baby boy—who all died shortly after birth.

My father was at work at the Southern Oil Cotton Company in Montgomery on the day that I was born, June 21, 1943. At the time, the black workers were trying to organize and they had chosen my father to be their spokesperson. He went to see the foreman on behalf of the black workers in the oil mill, and asked that they all get a raise in pay. Not surprisingly, the foreman didn't take this well. It was bad enough that the blacks were organizing, but to have my father come into his office and make a request like this was unthinkable. Retribution was swift.

The mill had a series of big boilers. There were two or three people shoveling coal in each one in order to keep the fires going. The foreman transferred my father to the midnight shift, where he had to stoke all the boilers by himself. That night he was on this new detail, trying to keep all of the boilers stoked, when the lights went out—all of them. It was pitch black except for the flickering orange light of the boiler fires. There he was, standing in the dark, not sure what to do, when he heard the voices.

"We're going to kill you," they chanted. He knew he was hearing the voice of the Ku Klux Klan.

He ran the three miles back home, told my mother to get things in order and headed for Chicago. He just jumped on a bus and headed north, knowing for certain that if he had stayed, he would have been killed. Although my father was always reluctant to admit that fact, my mother confirmed it years later.

A week later my mother, my older brother, my older sister, and I— only one month old—joined him. We lived in Chicago for five years, which turned out to be four tough years for my father. He hated big, cold, dirty Chicago, and longed to have the opportunity to return to Montgomery. He needed to be close to his family and close to his church. In Montgomery, he was a vital entity in his world. In Chicago, he felt as if he were just one from the masses.

When friends and family thought that it was safe enough to return to Alabama, we did so. My father's mother had taken ill and he urgently wanted to help take care of her. The move back was uneventful, as he never again had contact with the men who had meant to do him harm. He even went back to work at the old oil mill. He was happier, but no matter how much he enjoyed being back home, I believe that he knew then that another move would become necessary not too far down the road.

Five years later, in 1953, we moved to Detroit in search of a better life.

$\sim$

We moved into a house at 4125 St. Antoine Street on the east side of Detroit. It was just north of the infamous Brewster housing projects and one block west of Hastings Street, where you could find just about anything you wanted, legal or illegal. Many businesses lined Hastings, and it was filled with people nearly twenty-four hours a day. There were restaurants, movie theaters, clubs, pimps, prostitutes, and people running numbers. It was a vibrant, flourishing, and colorful neighborhood. It was a community, and even though there was liquor, prostitution, and numbers, it was civil. I never heard anyone swear. Everyone respected each other, and behaved honorably, especially in front of the youngsters.

There was a pool hall on the corner of Alexander and Hastings called Joe's Tap Room. The young guys used to hang around outside the front door and watch the adults shoot pool, all the while admiring the way they dressed with their snappy Stacy Adams or Ben B. Burke shoes and their Slim Stingy Brim hats. You could hear people remarking about how "clean" they were. Up the street was the Tip Top Grill, well known for their spiced ham sandwiches. Everybody went there and ate them, though some preferred the big greasy hamburgers. They had a great jukebox that was a nickel a play. It was there that I first heard Bill Doggett's big hit, "Honky Tonk."

The Willis Theater was across the street, and it showed second- and third-run movies. On the adjacent corner was Reverend C.L. Franklin's world famous New Bethel Baptist Church. A few blocks west, at Canfield and John R, was another place we loved to stand outside—the Flame Show Bar. Every black act that was big at the time played there, including Dinah Washington and Brook Benton.

It was a neighborhood filled with characters, like the man who sold watermelons during the summer, riding his horse-drawn wagon while calling out, "Boys and girls, stop playing in the sand. Go tell your mamma it's the watermelon man!" over and over at the top of his lungs. Of course we'd run in the house and tell our parents and they'd go outside and thump the watermelons until they found one they liked. He'd sell out in no time flat.

Life was fun in Detroit for a boy of ten. My friends and I played, doing the normal things that kids do, never realizing that we were poor or that there was a difference in where and how we lived compared to other people. Television wasn't big back then, so our exposure was limited. Sure, we went to the movies, but we knew that wasn't real life. We were just a bunch of young boys—and some girls—whose lives seemed to revolve around sports and hanging out in front of somebody's house. Every day we'd play something—basketball, football, baseball, it didn't matter. We just had a good time.

Much of the time, we'd play baseball at our grade school, Lincoln Elementary, which is now Spain Middle School near the Medical Center. The kids from Alexandrine Street would join with us and play against the kids from Superior Street. A neighborhood rite of passage was being able to hit a home run over the left field fence at Lincoln School. There was no fence in right field, it was just the wall of the school, so it had to be a home run over the fence in left. Even the left-handed batters would try to hit the ball over the fence, which was much harder than it was for us righties. It was just that important. To hit the ball over the fence was to be a man. The older guys from the neighborhood would sit around and watch us, waiting to find out who would be the next to join their ranks. People would stand and watch from their porches across the street from the park, waiting to find out who would be the next to join their ranks. We would watch each other anxiously, waiting to find out who would be the next to join their ranks. Fortunately, I was the first of the kids in my neighborhood to do it. When I was thirteen years old I hit a nice shot over the left field fence and was invited to join the men when they played on Sunday evenings. It was quite an honor. As I said, it was just that important.

Some of these friends continued in sports, like Richard Dickerson, Dickie to us. He was the greatest athlete in the neighborhood and went on to play in the American Basketball Association. Some of us did well, some ended up in jail, and others died young. The names of young men like Lonnie and Bobby and Red and Ralph are still very much imprinted in my mind and will reside there forever. They were the unlucky ones. They were good kids who were led astray at some point, either by drugs or gangs or an attempt to get some fast money. It saddens me to think about them and think about what could have been, but it also strengthens my resolve to help keep similar kids on track today. Nonetheless, they were my childhood friends and it was definitely an interesting neighborhood to grow up in.

Race was never a big issue for us. The neighborhood was about as far from being mixed as you could get. Maybe it was because we were kids, but we didn't make a big deal out of race. Everyone in our neighborhood looked like us and talked like us; the truth was that we just didn't think much about it.

One day, when I was twelve, Willie Mayo and I rode our bikes up past Harper Hospital, which is now considered the medical center. We came across two white kids from Georgia named Arnold and David and, kids being kids, we started talking. This was the first time that I'd ever interacted and played with white guys, and we became fast friends. They'd come over to my house, causing everybody in the neighborhood to look. There were very few white people who ever just came to my neighborhood to visit. There simply wasn't that type of interaction between the races back then. The only whites my neighbors and I were used to seeing were bill collectors, salespeople, and police officers. Although my neighbors really didn't care about my having white guys over to visit, they were just apprehensive about any two white guys. It wasn't that they had done anything or would do anything, but the apprehension would always exist.

~

My father was a slight man with huge, muscular arms that would remind you of Popeye. He was a laborer without a formal education, having only completed the second grade, and always worked at least two jobs. He grew up on a farm in Union Springs, Alabama, where at one time his family owned a great deal of land. Around the turn of the century the land was taken from them. I never learned why.

I only knew one of my grandparents, and that was my grandmother Ada. She was born in 1862 into slavery and died when she was 91 years old. She and my grandfather, Emmanuel, had my father and three daughters, Willie Pearl, Ada, and Ruth. I never got to see much of my aunts because we lived in Detroit and they were in Alabama, but we'd talk by phone from time to time. For years, my father, who didn't feel comfortable about his writing, dictated a weekly letter to his surviving sister that I'd write for him. Every letter was basically the same, and opened "Dear Willie"—never sister, always "Dear Willie"—"this leaves all of us doing well. I hope that you and your family are also well." And then he'd proceed to tell her about the family or the church—it was pretty much the same letter every week.

I thought it was a pain. Here I was a young kid and I had to sit down and write a letter for my dad. It didn't occur to me until years later that he was probably just as uncomfortable as I was, and that he may also have been doing it largely to help me become a better writer. But looking back at it now, it's a fond memory of something that we always did together.

There was another thing that we always did together—work. No matter where he worked, Dodge Main or Peerless Chemical, my father always had carpentry jobs on the side. For years, I was his assistant, which allowed us to spend a great deal of time together—time to learn carpentry, time to talk, time to just be father and son. He'd talk about the Bible, he'd talk about our family, and he'd talk about honesty, integrity, and sincerity. For all the talking we did—and let me tell you, over the years, I heard him say a lot—he never uttered a swear word or showed resentment toward anybody. He was a very fair person, in spite of some of the serious racial and segregationist times he experienced growing up in the South. He firmly believed there was good in every person, and that you shouldn't hate or dislike someone because of the color of his or her skin.

When I was thirteen years old my grandmother died. My father, my brother Cota, his wife Hilda, and I drove to Montgomery, Alabama for the funeral. Sunday night after the funeral we began our return trip back to Detroit. I'll never forget what happened next. It was about midnight and we were an hour north of Birmingham when my father noticed a car quickly pulling up behind us. "That sucker's really moving," he said as the car's high beams flashed on and off, indicating that they wanted to pass. My father pulled over as far right as he could to give the car plenty of room to pass, but they only mimicked us by driving to the right, staying right on our tail. He then pulled into the left lane to let the car pass on the right. As he did, they pulled alongside us and tried to force us into oncoming traffic.

If we slowed down, they slowed down. If we sped up, they sped up. I looked over and saw six young white men in the car, a 1953 Ford. I couldn't believe the looks on their faces. It was the first time that I had ever been confronted with this type of open hostility and I didn't know what to make of it—until I saw their faces. They were drinking and laughing and it was clear they meant to do us harm. It is difficult to understand the fear unless you've experienced it. Just as my fear reached its highest degree, I saw the stern look on my father's face underneath his glasses and the fear began to melt away. All of a sudden, I had total confidence that he was in complete control of the situation. The look on his face made it clear that nothing was going to happen to his family. My father was going to fight to the death for us.

As I woke up my brother, my father instructed him to get the tire iron from under the front seat. "Sonny," he said to me. "You use the baseball bat." He told Hilda to lock the doors and stay in the car no matter what.

"If you have to swing, don't swing wildly," he told us. "Conserve your energy and let's stand back-to-back, understand?"

I'd never seen this side of my father before. He was like a general preparing for battle. He watched the road. He planned. Suddenly we were being pelted with bricks and bottles. We slowed down and they followed suit. We turned into a Shell gas station and they were right behind us. They jumped out wielding bottles and sticks, trying to get in our car. My father stomped on the gas and we flew out of there.

"I left Alabama thinking I could get away from this," my father said. "And here I am in the middle of it again." I was extremely proud that my father had gotten us out of it without getting into a fight, though I know he always regretted the fact that the incident had occurred at all. He never talked about it again.

～

A lot of the talking my father and I did while working at those carpentry jobs was about his days playing baseball in the old Negro League. He'd been a catcher, and he spoke glowingly of the fact that he caught for players like Leroy "Satchel" Paige, though he told me time and again that the greatest pitcher he ever caught for was a man by the name of Booker T. Brunion.

"Satchel Paige was great, and he could throw hard and move the ball around," he'd say while we were banging nails. "But I'm telling you, this Booker T. Brunion, he was the greatest pitcher I ever saw. This guy had a curveball you wouldn't believe. Why, we'd line up three barrels between home plate and the pitcher's mound and Booker T. would throw that ball and it would curve between the barrels and slide right over the plate smooth as honey."

As a kid I believed every word of it, but as I got older I started to doubt that it was possible. "Come on, Pop, he didn't really do that between three barrels."

"No, you're right," he'd say with a smile. "It was actually two!" And we'd laugh.

The older I got, the more skeptical I grew of my father's athletic background. After all, I'd never seen him play ball. I didn't call him a liar to his face—I'd never have done that—but I started to doubt whether he'd really been as good as he claimed to be.

The first time I got a chance to discover the truth was when I was at Cass Technical High School in 1957. I wanted to pitch for the baseball team, and even though I had a strong arm the coach said that I'd never be a pitcher unless I developed a good curveball. My older brother Cody tried to teach me, but it just wasn't working. We were practicing next to the house one day when my father came out to watch. "Sonny, let me show you how to throw a curveball," he said. He took the ball, wound up, and with a snap of his wrist, let the ball fly toward my brother. It rose and then fell in a downward diagonal across the imaginary home plate. Cody stabbed at it but missed.

"Do that again, Pop," I said, amazed at what I'd just seen. The next pitch he threw curved even more.

"Show me how," I begged. And he did.

In 1968, I had a chance to discover the real truth about my father's baseball years. The Harlem Globetrotters were in Detroit performing at Olympia Stadium. At halftime, they brought out a very special guest— none other than Satchel Paige himself. I was a police officer then and was on duty at the stadium. Since I had access, I went into the back to talk to Mr. Paige afterward.

"Excuse me, Mr. Paige," I said.

He saw my police uniform and smiled. "Yes sir?"

"Please don't call me sir," I said. Here I was about twenty-five years old and this famous man who was at least three times my age was calling me "Sir"! "Can I ask you a question?"

"You can ask me anything you want as long as it's not about my mother!" he joked.

"Tell me, did you ever play ball with a man in Alabama by the name of McKinnon?"

"What was that name again?"

"McKinnon," I repeated. "It would have been back in the twenties."

He wiped his brow. He was thinking, really searching, trying hard to remember. "Son," he said. "I played ball in so many places and with so many people...no, I don't think so."

My heart sank. In that one moment, I had caught my father in a big lie. Not only hadn't he ever played with Satchel Paige, but he probably wasn't the great catcher he always claimed that he'd been.

"Thanks," I said sadly, as I turned to walk away.

"Wait a minute, son," he said. I was almost out the door. "What did you say that man's name was again?"

"McKinnon."

"McKinnon...Cota McKinnon."

My eyes lit up!

"He was a catcher. Used to catch for a pitcher by the name of Booker T. Brunion."

"That's my father!" I exclaimed.

"Oh yeah," he said. "I remember Cota McKinnon. I played ball against him down in Alabama. He used to talk a blue streak to the batters. We called him Motor Mouth." He laughed. "You know something, son, he was one of the greatest ball players I ever saw."

You can't imagine how I felt when Satchel Paige—*the* Satchel Paige—told me that my father was a great baseball player. He told me about how my father played against him, played against Josh Gibson, even played against the white major leaguers when they came down to Alabama.

"Son, let me tell you something about your daddy." He kept calling him my daddy. "He was good enough to play in the major leagues, and he would have if the color line had been broken then. Yes sir, your daddy was good alright. He could have made a career of it except he wouldn't barnstorm. He wanted to stick close to his family."

A tear came to my eye. One of the greatest baseball players of all time validated everything my father had told me. I was so proud that I almost floated out of Olympia Stadium. I went right home to tell my father.

"Pop!" I called out as I ran into the house. "Guess who I met today?"

"Who?"

"Satchel Paige."

"And," he asked matter of factly, "did he tell you?"

"Yes, Pop, he did. He told me what a great baseball player you were, what a great catcher you were, what a great arm you had..."

Mr. Paige didn't have to tell me what a great father I had.

∼

I was a lot like my father in that I always worked. I'd pick up pop bottles in the street and take them back for the deposit. I'd collect scrap metal and take it to the junkyard. I delivered newspapers, shoveled snow, and worked in Mrs. McCoy's market. It was always something. But one of the more lucrative professions that I had as a young boy was shining shoes. I learned to do this while working at a barbershop on Hastings Street where I swept the floors for $10 a week and shined shoes on the side. I also had my one and only fling with criminal life there.

Every day the barber would hand me a big bag and tell me to take it over to a house on Illinois Street. I took this to be a part of my duties at the shop and never gave it a thought, until one day I told my mother about it and she said, "Sonny, the next time you do that, look in the bag." Sure enough, the next day I peeked inside and it was filled with betting slips. Now my mother, like most people in the neighborhood, played the numbers, but she didn't want her son getting drawn into anything illegal, so she made me quit. But that was fine with me, because while I was there I'd been prepped for my next career—shining shoes.

My father, who always encouraged me to be a go-getter, built a shoeshine stand for me in front of our house on St. Antoine. It had seats for two people and was beautiful. Well, except for the paint job, which was this incredible bright pink color. Being eleven years old, I was mortified.

"Son, this is our gimmick," he told me. "People will be interested in this pink shoeshine stand. They'll notice it. They'll talk about it. Word will spread and you'll get lots of business."

My friends teased me unmercifully. At least until the first Saturday that I was open for business and a steady stream of customers showed up. At about 4:00, I checked my money and I had taken in five bucks—at ten cents a crack! The word spread about this pink shoeshine stand and my business increased steadily until I was taking in as much as $10 a day. At my father's urging, I raised my price to twenty-five cents. And why not? He was right about the bright pink color attracting people, wasn't he? And attract people it did. On Sunday mornings the deacons from the New Bethel and New Bethlehem Baptist churches would line up four or five deep waiting for a shoeshine. I was making $20 a week—half as much as most adults in the neighborhood—and I was only eleven!

One thing I learned early on was that whatever you made, you always gave part of it back to your family. If I made $20 shining shoes, I'd give $18 to my family. If I made $5 returning pop bottles, I'd give $4 to my mother. Of course, the other couple of bucks was mine to do whatever I wanted to with, and more often than not, I'd go to the movies. The Willis Theater, which was on Hastings Street, showed B-movies, which back in the '50s meant mostly cowboy flicks. Then there were the second-run the-aters on Woodward—the Roxy, the Colonial, and the Fine Arts Theater. I'd use the money to take my sisters Gloria and Helen to a movie almost every day. After all, it was a chance to escape and really enjoy ourselves, seeing movies that eventually became the classics: "Casablanca," "Shane," "High Noon," oh, and anything with Edward G. Robinson or James Cagney.

∾

Naturally, my parents were the strongest influences on my life. But there were several other people who played a big part in my development.

One of the most influential was Raymond Hughes, my woodshop teacher at Garfield Junior High School. He'd have long conversations with me and the other boys about life, instilling the idea that it was important for us to strive to succeed, telling us how we should work hard to ensure that anything we did we did right. This was quite a revelation. While my father demonstrated many of these same lessons, he never actually sat me down and told me straight on. It wasn't until many years later that I realized that both of them were telling me very much the same thing, but in different ways. I also realized that if every young man had had the opportunity to be involved with my father and Mr. Hughes, their lives would have been exponentially better off because of it. I consider myself very lucky because of them, and I'm certain that I've modeled my life after them and after others who have striven to make a difference in people's lives.

In the case of Mr. Hughes, it was especially impressive that he was doing this after school, on his own time, often spending a couple of hours a day with us just because he wanted to help the boys in the neighborhood.

Over the years, I kept in touch with him as he moved up the ladder. And as he did, he never stopped making an impact on kids' lives. He continually embraced the idea of being a role model as he became a principal at one of the high schools and I went on to become chief of police. One day I received a call from someone at his school notifying me that Mr. Hughes was retiring. He asked if I'd come and speak at his retirement luncheon. I was ecstatic, and I was honored.

The luncheon was held in Warren, Michigan, and a number of my former teachers were present. Even though I was 53 years old and the chief of police, I instantly reverted to "Yes, ma'am" and "No, sir" just as if I were still in class. It was wonderful that I had an opportunity to tell them about the profound impact Mr. Hughes had on my life and to publicly thank him for it. And being as modest as he was selfless, he was just embarrassed by the praise.

The second person who significantly influenced my life was Mr. Bunche, who I later found out was a relative of Ralph Bunche, the first black man to win the Nobel Peace Prize. I never knew his first name. To me he was always just Mr. Bunche. He was a slender man who owned a coal yard on Superior Street, right around the corner from our house, and I used to help him out by making deliveries. I'd get ten cents for each bushel of coal I delivered, no matter whether I took it around the corner or all the way to the Brewster Projects. I'd pull my wagon filled with two bushels of coal from home to home.

One day, as I returned from a delivery, I heard an unusual noise coming from the shed that was his office.

"What's that?" I asked as I stepped inside.

He looked at me, amazed. "What do you mean 'What is that?'"

"I mean, what's that noise?" I asked.

"Son, you mean to tell me you don't know what that is?"

"No sir, I don't."

Now he was staring at me. "Son, that's classical music."

He asked if I'd ever heard of Marian Anderson and I said No. Paul Robeson? No. Mario Lanza? No.

Mr. Bunche must have realized at that moment that I had a very limited knowledge of the world outside the neighborhood. So he locked the gate to the coal yard and took me to the main library on Woodward Avenue. He marched me upstairs to the second floor, where you could put headphones on and listen to record albums.

"Do you know what this is?" he asked.

"Yeah, sure," I told him. "That's the Lone Ranger theme."

"No, Isaiah, that's the William Tell Overture. This music is important, to you and to everyone. You need to learn about music and the people behind it!"

He played all kinds of music for me, much of it familiar after having heard it in the movies. And when the music ended, he would try his best to fill in other gaps. He taught me the history of black people, which I wasn't learning in school. He told me about Haile Selassie and Harriet Tubman. He taught me that Crispus Attucks, a black man, was the first person killed in the Revolutionary War. He told me what black people were doing in other parts of the United States and around the world, giving me my first lessons in the history of black people in this country. And he quizzed me relentlessly until I could name the capital of every state in the country and every country in the world.

He was unlike any other man I had ever met, since very few black men at the time had the background that Mr. Bunche had. He had traveled, and he always talked about his travels. He talked about where he had been, what he had seen, and what he hoped to see in the future. He talked about life in a way that made it exciting and filled with potential, and piqued my interest about what was happening outside of Detroit. Here was this little starry-eyed kid sitting before him and he wanted to answer every question I had. He saw that I wanted to learn, so he taught me.

Then one day he did the most incredible thing. "I talked to your mother," he said. "And tonight you and I are going to the Rackham Memorial Building."

I knew the Rackham Memorial Building. It was in the Cultural Center near the library, right across the street from the museum. I asked him what we were going to do there.

"We're going to see the University of Michigan Orchestra," he said with a smile.

That night we sat in the audience, the only two blacks in a sold out crowd. There I was, a young impressionable kid from inner city Detroit. I took everything in, and even though I felt strange about being such a minority, it was counterbalanced when I saw and heard the incredible orchestra music! These were instruments that I'd heard but never seen, music that I'd listened to on record that was now actually being performed live. For me!

All through my life I've had a passion for music. I love all kinds, from pop to classical, Broadway show tunes to country and western. I've sung in choirs and in rock bands. I've sung for children and backstage with Johnny Mathis. And I owe it all to the fact that Mr. Bunche took the time to open up a whole new world of education to a young neighborhood boy.

Mr. Bunche and Mr. Hughes were just two uncommon people who took the time to share.

CHAPTER *two*

After graduating from Cass Technical High School in 1961, I enlisted in the United States Air Force and began a four-year stint as a machinist. In the neighborhood I grew up in, the military was the first option of employment to prepare a young man for the transition from high school to the factory. Most of us saw college as a remote dream, far from reality. It was a matter of natural order to either go to the military, to the factory, or to jail.

Other than being beaten by Rotation Slim when I was fourteen years old, I'd encountered very little racism until I got to Lackland Air Force Base in San Antonio, Texas for basic training. I became the leader of a flight, which is what the Air Force calls a squadron. This wasn't a promotion—they just picked out someone who they thought might be able to handle being a little in charge and threw him to the wolves. We were a mixed group, mostly from Michigan, Georgia, Alabama, and a few from New Hampshire. Out of sixty-five men in my flight, seven were black, so you can imagine the dynamics. The military tries to train you to think and be as one, not to see race or other differences. Unfortunately, this is easier said than done.

My first racial encounter occurred when a black airman made a comment to a white counterpart about not liking the work assignment he'd drawn.

"Listen up, you niggers in this flight," the white airman announced. "Don't you be complaining. We don't even need you around here 'cause you ain't no good."

A very serious physical confrontation ensued, I'd never fought anyone over a racial remark before, but for some reason I really laid into him.

I fought with a violence I never knew was inside me.

Our sergeant, a white guy from Massachusetts named Martel, disciplined the white airman and praised me and other blacks for the way we stood up. But even though he was telling me that I had done the right thing, I couldn't help but be upset by how violent I had gotten. That was a side of me that I had never seen before and hoped I would never see again.

A second incident occurred one Saturday when a group of us got eight-hour passes and went into town. We came across a theater where "Spartacus" was playing and I wanted to go in and see it. The other guys were more interested in a different kind of entertainment—one that involved women. They pooled their money to see if they could afford it. Or maybe to see how many women they could afford. I'm not sure. Personally, I was more interested in the movie.

Lynn, a white friend from Ohio, also wanted to see the movie, so the two of us got in line. Lynn bought his ticket first. Then I got mine and the ticket seller told me I had to go through the side door and sit in the balcony.

"Excuse me?" I asked, not sure that I had heard her correctly.

"He can go in this door and sit downstairs," she said, referring to Lynn. "But coloreds have to go in the side door and sit in the balcony."

I couldn't believe I was hearing this. I mean, there I was in uniform, ready to defend her and her country, and she was insisting that I had to go around the side and sit in the balcony. "You gotta be kidding!"

The funny part was that she probably couldn't believe it was happening either.

"Do you see this uniform?" I asked her. "I'm in the Air Force."

"It doesn't matter. Colored people don't sit downstairs with the whites."

I demanded my money back. Disgusted, Lynn did too. The cashier threw our money at us and we stormed off. When we got back to the base we complained to the sergeant. He apologized, saying, "That's the way this place is. And I hate to tell you this, but there are going to be other places like this too."

I never went back into San Antonio. Instead I stayed on the base and bided my time until I completed my basic training and was shipped out. I had heard about, but had never seen first-hand, racial problems that were that serious—and that prevalent. It made me pay close attention to black people who lived in the community. I started talking to them about their problems and concerns. It was a real eye-opener.

After San Antonio, I was shipped out to Minot, North Dakota, where I got another quick lesson about life and people. I traveled by train from Detroit to Chicago, then on to Minneapolis and Bismarck. From there, I took a bus to Minot. It was a part of the country I'd never seen, and I loved the trip. At least until I got to Minot, where I found myself stuck with no bus to the base, which was located about twenty-five miles outside of town. I called the base and they told me to take a taxi or hitchhike. Being a city boy from Detroit, I'd never hitchhiked before, but I was game, so I stood out in front of the bus station in my Air Force blue uniform and considered how to go about this. I hadn't stuck my thumb out or done anything when a green car pulled up with four young white men in it.

"What the hell are you doing here, nigger?" they yelled.

There I was, standing on the street of a strange town, and it was happening to me again. I didn't even answer them. I just walked back into the bus station and called a taxi. I was learning.

The next day, I went through the personnel process, something you do on the first day of any new assignment in the military. I had already cleared most of the areas and was walking from the medical section when a car pulled up. It was a green car. It was the same green car filled with the same four guys from the night before.

"Hey!" they called out. "Why don't you take your black ass back home?"

Now remember this was a United States Air Force base and I was a member of the Armed Forces. It was like some bad dream. I picked up a brick and I heaved it at the car as they sped off.

This time I went to my commanding officer, a salt-and-pepper-haired, spit-and-polish major who looked every bit the part. He looked genuinely concerned as I told him about the incidents in San Antonio and the one here. I confided in him about how I felt, about the hurt, the confusion.

"Airman, there are always going to be people who think and behave like those idiots," he told me. "But you'll find that the majority of the people in this world aren't like that. And never will be. So put it behind you and move on with life."

There was something about this hard, tough military man offering such reassuring words that reached me. I took his words to heart. There is racism everywhere. Period. Even today, I wish I were able to truly understand the core of the racist mind, but I don't think there is anyone that can. Racist negativity is a cancer that seems to linger in the minds of some, and I wish I had the magic wand to enlighten them. But there simply is no magic wand.

As long as the idiots who think and talk and act upon their racism keep thinking and talking and acting the way they do, their voice will seem larger than it actually is. They'll keep their starring roles in the media and they'll intimidate the "neutral" people, who I am confident make up the majority. The cure is for the other "neutral" people to stand up and let it be known they're simply not going to accept that kind of behavior anymore.

I don't.

~

The racial tensions in Minot were much the same as in Texas. The permanent residents in the area looked down on the Native Americans. The heavily rural and southern soldiers looked down on blacks, Hispanics, Asians, and Native Americans—basically, anyone who didn't look like them. Everyone seemed to have an ethnic group to look down on.

The pecking order on the base was clearly defined and deeply ingrained. Most of the ranking officers were white southerners, while the majority of the blacks worked in supply, a nonskilled position. A few were assigned to the Air Police. Maybe I was fortunate to have been educated as a machinist after my training at Cass Technical High School. It was a major disappointment that in the military, people weren't given the same opportunities and were instead segregated by skill levels.

The civil rights movement was growing. More urban northern blacks were joining the military, and they weren't taking the same guff southern blacks had taken, so naturally there were more conflicts. When Dr. Martin Luther King went to Washington, D.C. and gave his "I Have a Dream" speech at the Washington Mall, the comments of the whites on the base were predictable. They said he was a communist sympathizer leading people to Washington who should have been back home looking for jobs and work.

I had admired Dr. King for years and wanted to go to the Lincoln Memorial, where he gave his famous speech. I finally got my chance in 1977, the first time I went to the FBI Academy in Quantico, Virginia for special training. A fellow officer, who'd also been in the Air Force, and I went to the Lincoln Memorial on a hot summer weekend. It was a very moving experience. As I stood beneath Abraham Lincoln, I looked out and pictured Dr. King in that very place fourteen years before, with thousands of people packed in the mall listening to him say, "I have a dream that my four little children will one day live in a nation where they will not be judged by the color of their skin but by the content of their character. I have a dream today." I wish I could have been there, been a part of that historic moment.

~

The Cold War was still going strong. The Strategic Air Command was the backbone of the nation's defense, and they kept B-52 bombers and KC-135 refueling planes in the air twenty-four hours a day. We maintained these aircraft and missiles at Minot Air Force Base. One day we were put on alert, which meant that if you lived on base you couldn't leave, and if you lived off base you were restricted to going to and from your home. We had no idea what was going on, but we very much understood the importance and urgency. We figured there was a problem with the Russians, or maybe a Chinese–Indian border skirmish. Everyone was tense, not knowing what was going on, wondering if we were preparing to go to war. It was the Cuban Missile Crisis.

I have to admit that hindsight has made the underlying incidents around this day clearer to me. In the Strategic Air Command, our motto was "Peace is Our Profession," and we took a lot of pride in that. This pride seemed to be misguided that day as we watched on television as President Kennedy put the blockade in place, issuing the ultimatum to Khrushchev and the Russians. There was an air of macho nationalism in the room as we just sat there and waited for war. I remember listening to some guys who were talking about the "Monroe Doctrine" and stating that we had the right to blow the Russians back to kingdom come. We never thought of the consequences—they were going to do the same dog-gone thing to us. Thank God Khrushchev blinked and backed down. If he hadn't, I firmly believe that 75 percent of the people of the world would have lost their lives that day.

In June of 1964, after about three years in Minot, I received my transfer orders: I was being shipped out to a little known place called Vietnam. They gave me fifteen days of leave, so I went home to see my family. Then I reported to Travis Air Force Base just outside of San Francisco where I had a two-day layover before the twenty-four-hour flight to Vietnam. I'd never been to San Francisco, so I knew I needed to check out the town. After all, it had one of the best reputations going.

I stayed at the Governor Hotel for about $15 a night. When I checked in, the desk clerk noticed my uniform and asked if I wanted a blonde, brunette, or redhead in my room.

"What?" I asked, certain that I hadn't heard him right.

"Which would you prefer? A blonde, brunette, or redhead?"

"Do they come with the room?"

He shook his head and went about finishing up the check-in. Obviously, we weren't as worldly in Detroit as they were in San Francisco. I spent my days seeing the sights of the city and fell in love with it. How could you not? It's a beautiful city and, like everyone who visits, I heard Tony Bennett singing "I Left My Heart in San Francisco" in an endless loop in my head. If there were another city where I would have lived besides Detroit, it would have been this beautiful city by the bay. My wife and sons have also fallen in love with it.

Two weeks later, after a brief jungle training session in the Philippines, I was in Saigon.

CHAPTER *three*

M y first words as my feet hit the tarmac were, "This has got to be what hell is like. I'll never survive this heat." It was the summer of 1964 and we weren't officially at war yet. We were there as advisors to the South Vietnamese, though, and with 27,000 American soldiers in the country there was no question that some of the Special Forces and Marines were fighting.

Saigon was beautiful. It wasn't called the Paris of the Orient for nothing. GIs were everywhere, though almost no one carried a gun. The guys who had been there for a while showed the new transferees around, taking us to Cholon, the central Chinese area, where most of the GIs hung out. It was a real eye-opener for someone like me who had never spent any time outside of the United States. No sooner would you step into a bar than a young woman would walk up to you and say, "I love you GI. You number one. You buy for me whiskey Coke?" For fifty piastres—about twenty-five cents—you could buy a drink. Then naturally you would get one for yourself. That was the idea, since they were bar girls who were being paid for each drink they got a GI to buy. They would be served colored water or something equally innocuous. The GIs did slightly better—we'd get watered down drinks. Except for me. I got the real thing, since I drank Coca Colas—but only for a while. When rumor spread that they put embalming fluid in Cokes, I stopped drinking them too.

Most of the bar girls weren't prostitutes; they were just extremely poor women who came down from the mountains or out of the slums and were trying to make a living. They did pretty well—especially on military payday when the guys would rush downtown to spend their money as fast as they could. It was fun in its own way. We were away from home, so why not act out these little games and be something of a fool? When you are overseas, such as we were, you tended to act out trying to forget the fact that you might at any time lose your life. Of course, there were always other factors, and some GIs took full advantage of the circumstances, but it was almost a necessity to vent in these ways.

After a few days in Saigon, I boarded a C-123 plane to my final destination: Da Nang. It's about 380 miles northeast of Saigon and about 100 miles from the DMZ, or demilitarized zone. It was beautiful—sweltering, but beautiful. Each branch of the military had its own living area in Da Nang. We lived in tents until a typhoon blew them all away. After that, we stayed in barracks that were screened-in on the sides and had a vague semblance of a roof overhead. If you didn't sleep under mosquito netting you'd be eaten alive, and considering how we ate, the mosquitoes were getting the better meals. We had roast beef practically every day. We drank powdered milk, both chocolate and regular. The chocolate milk ended up kind of syrupy and the white milk would make you constipated. If you regulated how much of each you drank you could keep yourself pretty regular.

There wasn't a lot to do there, so we would usually drink in the evening. Not being much of a drinker, I stuck to my favorite, grape soda pop. One night some of the guys and I were hanging out in a club that we had built —and believe me, calling it a club is being very complimentary. I was with five good old southern boys who were drinking straight shots, at a cost of about a dime apiece. After a while they got to teasing me about drinking grape pop. I held up for a while, but eventually it started to get to me.

"Hey, I can drink," I protested. And drink I did.

I ordered a whiskey and Coke. Then another. And another. They'd drink one, and I'd match them. This was the first and only time in my life that I had ever done this, and I ended up drinking twelve whiskey and Cokes. It didn't seem to be affecting them, and I thought I was doing well. I was proud of myself for having remembered that it was good to eat if you drank. I nibbled on bread the entire time. At some point I started to see double. Then I thought there was steam coming out of my ears. I told them I'd had enough.

They died laughing as good old straightlaced Ike stumbled down the street trying to find his way home. As luck would have it, I ran into the chaplain, who looked at me and asked, "Airman McKinnon, are you all right?" I have no idea what I said to him in response. I only know that somehow I made it back to my bunk and fell asleep. Amazingly, I didn't wake up with a hangover, but I swore that I wasn't going to do that again. Believe me, the guys tried. They joked that they were going to have me drinking liquor, smoking cigarettes, and chugging coffee by the time I went back to the states. But they were wrong. I'd learned my lesson.

There were two guys I hung around with a lot while I was in Vietnam. Their names were Haron Rayles and Dick—I only knew him as Dick. Haron was a big black guy who stood about 6-foot-5 and Dick was a short white guy with a heavy southern accent. We made quite a trio. We'd go downtown and hop from bar to bar, each one filled with GIs drinking, buying drinks for the bar girls, and listening to music. I don't know how they did it, but the bars always had the most recent American music. The first time I heard the Righteous Brothers was at the New York Bar in Da Nang. A guy we called Pig—because he was big and, well, looked like a pig—called me over and told me to listen to the song that was playing.

"You've lost that lovin' feeling. Whoa, that lovin' feeling. You've lost that loving' feeling, now it's gone, gone, gone. And I can't go on, Whoa-oa-oa."

"Who do you think that is?" he asked.

"I don't know."

"Listen. Who do you think that is?"

I realized he wasn't asking me who the group was, but rather if they were black or white. "They're black," I told him.

"No, no, man, they're two white dudes."

I was shocked to hear that they were white, and even more shocked about what I saw in the weeks that followed. It was the first time I had ever heard a white group that sounded like a black one, and I began to see some of the black GIs singing that Righteous Brothers song all around the base. Now this may seem insignificant now, but at the time it was terribly important. It blurred a line of preference and separation that had never been blurred before. Everyone knew the song, and everyone sang the song. So credit the Righteous Brothers with opening at least one door for race relations in the 1960s.

Music was important to us. You'd walk into a bar and more often than not hear a roomful of guys harmonizing to a song, especially if they were playing "It's All Right" by the Impressions. That was *the* song—*"It's all right. Have a good time, 'cause it's all right. Wow, wow, it's all right."* —Even though I didn't drink, I'd go to the bars just to have a good time. A lot of the others were more interested in drinking and finding a girl for a dollar or two, but I stuck to my pals and my grape pop.

One night Dick, Haron, and I were sitting in the New York Bar. Dick was talking to a young lady and must have said something that didn't sit well with her, because she motioned to a Vietnamese guy at the bar, who apparently was her boyfriend or husband. He was a member of the ARVN, the Army Republic of Vietnam, and while the GIs went downtown unarmed, the ARVN carried their weapons. He walked up to Dick and said something to him. Dick, knowing that most of the South Vietnamese men weren't great physical fighters, hit him, sending him flying out the door. All of a sudden the guy pulls a .45 caliber handgun out of his holster. I took off running, followed closely by Dick and Haron. As we rounded the corner, the guy started shooting at us, not caring about who he was aiming at. The Air Police, which is the Air Force version of MPs, showed up along with the QCs, who are the Vietnamese equivalent. They surrounded the guy with guns drawn. We were about a block away as we hightailed it out of there. The oddest thought hit me later: I could have been killed in a bar fight in Vietnam and people would have assumed that I had lost my life in some heroic way.

When you get a lot of GIs together the mix of testosterone and liquor can be explosive. One time I was in a bar with this 350-pound soldier called Tiny and another named Valentine, who had a very serious drinking problem. We were all talking, singing, and having a good time until Valentine made a comment about the size of Tiny's manhood. Not a good move. Especially after he repeated it. Tiny jumped up and swung at Valentine, missing him and hitting Dick. Dick swung back, and before you knew it they had all gotten into it. I did my best to calm them down and be the peacemaker until Tiny told me where to go. I jumped on his back. I was 220 pounds at the time, but he turned quickly and threw me across the room like I was a rag doll. I ran back and jumped on him again, only to be thrown off again. Then the Air Police showed up and I backed off—I didn't see any reason to get hurt in the mess.

"Okay, break it up. Break it up," one of the Air Police said. Tiny was oblivious to who they were, taking on anyone who got near him and not showing any sign of slowing down. "Okay, everybody step back. I got him," the overconfident A.P. declared.

Tiny stopped for a moment, looked at him and said, "Oh, you got me, huh?"

The A.P. swung at Tiny with his nightstick, smacking him hard on the head. Tiny stood there and smiled. "Oh, my god," the AP muttered just before Tiny lit into him. It took ten of us to wrestle Tiny to the ground so they could handcuff him. Of course, fighting wasn't a big offense there; it was just a part of military life in Vietnam.

Many of the Vietnamese chewed betel nuts, which gave them some kind of narcotic high and made their teeth black. One day I was in the mess hall talking to a guy named Jackson when this Vietnamese guy who worked there walked over and stood right next to our table chewing his betel nut, the black juice dripping from his mouth onto my plate.

"Oh, come on now!" I said, looking at the gross sight. *"Deedee!,"* I said, which means "Go away." He stood there, not moving, so I repeated it, *"Deedee! Deedee!"* His reply to me was, *"Come deedee,"* which meant that he was not going away.

Jackson thought this was funny and started laughing. "Man, this guy is on your case." So I said, *"Deedee, deedee mau!"* which means go away quickly.

"Come deedee," he repeated, being obstinate.

"Look you old son of a gun, *deedee. Deedee mau!"*

"Come deedee."

I stood up, grabbed him by the collar, and picked him up—all 130 pounds of him. I was carrying him through the mess hall to toss him outside when I heard someone scream, "Look out, Ike! He's got a knife!" Before I could do anything, he swung his arm at my stomach, stabbing at me. Lucky for me he had a dull table knife that hit my belt buckle and broke, or I might not be around today. I leaned back, swung, and tossed him into a big vat of soup.

The guy was screaming, the mess hall was in an uproar, and my sergeant, Joel Escovelle, came running at me yelling "Ike, what the hell are you doing?"

"This guy just tried to kill me, Sarge!"

"But why did you have to throw him in the soup?"

They fired the man but didn't press charges. The levity of the situation aside, this was one of my first brushes with death. GIs are brainwashed into thinking that nothing can happen or will happen to them, but this situation opened my eyes to the fact that I was terribly vulnerable in Vietnam. And although the realization of my vulnerability had a great deal of impact, it didn't change the fact that I had absolute confidence in myself and in my destiny. I knew that I was not sent to Vietnam to die. There was too much I needed to do with the rest of my life.

About a month later I was in downtown Da Nang when the Viet Cong started bombing the base. A group of us made a mad dash to get back, running through the side streets and alleys, staying as close to the houses as we could. Suddenly I looked up ahead and the Vietnamese guy who tried to stab me was standing in front of me, about 100 feet away. I stopped dead in my tracks, unsure of what to do.

He motioned to me, hands palm down, saying *"Liday! Liday!"* which I knew meant "come here quickly." I stared at him, not knowing whether to follow him or run from a possible trap. I looked into the man's eyes, and in a split second I decided to put my faith in him. He ran ahead, and I followed close behind, twisting and turning through streets and alleys that I never knew existed, leading us back to the base and to safety. I was frightened to see him, and if he had been a different type of person he might have killed me—but he didn't. It was as if he felt truly sorry about the day in the mess hall and wanted to make it up to me by going above and beyond. Without his help, I would have surely died in the bombing.

But, as I said before, it just wasn't my time. Needless to say, we got the man rehired, but I still wonder whether he knew what he was doing in the mess hall or whether he was too high from his betel nut to have had any idea what was going on. I choose to think it was the betel nut.

A highlight of my time in Da Nang was working with a Catholic priest, Father Shea, who helped build an orphanage for Vietnamese and Amerasian babies. The first time we went to the orphanage I noticed there were only nuns taking care of the children, no men. It was a very sad place with all these babies lying in their cribs, barely moving, obviously hungry, flies crawling in and out of their eyes, noses, and mouths. They weren't malnourished but they were very much underloved. It wasn't the fault of the nuns; there were just so many more babies than people to take care of them. The priest and I would go there on Saturdays and help out, mostly building things they needed and cleaning up the place. Father Shea tried to get more GIs involved, but it was pretty much a lost cause. I was impressed by how much he and the nuns cared. Their dedication and compassion were a great example to us all.

Life was tough in Vietnam. One of the people who really touched me during my 366 days there was an airman we called "Combat" Brown. He was a tall man, about 6'5", with very long arms. He hadn't run or exercised a day in his life, but he looked as though he'd been lifting weights since he was old enough to know what they were. He had this funny walk—he looked as though he were marching to a cadence. The nickname "Combat" came about because he crewed on the C-123 planes that dropped food into the jungle for the Special Forces troops and somehow his planes always seemed to get shot up more than anybody else's. We all joked about this, wondering why Combat's planes were always the ones to get shot at. "The V.C. can't kill me because I have too much class and per-sonality," he once told me. It got to a point where a number of the pilots were apprehensive about going out with Combat because it meant their planes would get shot up. He was considered a jinx.

We got friendly, and we certainly made an odd couple—I was straight-laced and didn't drink or smoke, but he consumed more than enough for the two of us. We would just sit and talk about life. He'd tell me about how he had failed in two marriages, and about how he always seemed to do the wrong thing. He regretted so many things he had done and felt especially bad about the people upon whom he had had a nega-tive impact. He just didn't know how to take care of himself or how to take care of his life, and I think I was drawn to him in order to take care of him. He was truly a unique person.

One night I was deep asleep when I awoke with a start—Combat was kneeling next to my bed. It had to have been 3:00 in the morning and he was in tears. "Ike…Ike…Ike…these mothers, they're trying to kill me."

"What are you talking about, Combat?"

"I'm supposed to go home next week but they extended my time by a month." Tears were rolling down his cheeks. "They're going to kill me, Ike. They're going to kill me. I've almost made it a year, but now they're going to kill me."

I had never seen him cry before. I listened to him and took him to see the chaplain. They talked, and Combat was shipped out a few days later. I felt really good about that, and I always wondered if I might have helped save his life.

∾

As soon as I was discharged from the Air Force and had returned to Detroit, I went to police headquarters to fulfill the pledge I had made to myself the day Rotation Slim had beaten me. Although I had received other offers and had briefly entertained thoughts of different paths, I never had a doubt that I was going to become a police officer. I needed to make my pledge a reality.

The recruiting office was in room 205, on the second floor of a large, dirty, gray building. No sooner had I stepped through the door than this wonderful man came rushing up to me. It was Avery Jackson, who turned out to be the only black person who worked in recruiting.

"Young man," he said brightly. "Can I help you?"

I told him that I wanted to sign up.

"Come on over here and have a seat," he said, leading me to his desk. "Tell me something about yourself."

After I gave him a brief history of my life, he asked if I had ever been arrested.

"No sir, I haven't."

"Any problems whatsoever?"

"No, sir."

During the course of our conversation, I told him that I'd won the Military Olympics twice in Da Nang. Beaming, he took me over to Inspector Quaid, who was in charge of recruiting and was also a great athlete. "I want to introduce you to Isaiah McKinnon. He wants to become a police officer. He won the Military Olympics while serving his country in Vietnam." One by one he took me around to each investigator in the office, saying the same thing, "I want to introduce you to Isaiah McKinnon. He wants to become a police officer." He played up all the angles: military, clean-cut, Cass Technical High School graduate, outstanding athlete.

Since Avery had "found" me, he would be the lead investigator, whose

responsibility it would be to look into my background. He interviewed
my parents and neighbors. Everyone told him that Sonny—which is what
they had all called me—was a wonderful boy, never a problem. Amazingly,
I didn't have to pay a one of them! I had a clean record, had just come out
of the military, and had never even gotten a traffic ticket or been arrested.
In fact, I had never even charged anything, so I didn't have a credit problem. So it wasn't too surprising that I came home one day to find a letter
waiting for me that read:

Dear Isaiah McKinnon:

You have been selected as a candidate for the Detroit Police Department.
Please report to 555 Clinton St. on August 2, 1965 at 7:30 am, where you will
be processed to become a Detroit police officer.

~

My class in the academy had more minorities than any in the history
of the Detroit police department. Out of sixty-five recruits, seven were
black, and one of them was female. Back then, women had to have a college degree to join the department, and even then they weren't allowed to
go on active patrol in the streets. Instead they were assigned to the Women's
Division, where they mostly handled cases that dealt with women, like
rape and domestic abuse.

The police department had a long history of abuse and neglect
toward blacks. Back in the '50s they were still able to hold people for up
to seventy-two hours under what was called investigative arrest—basically, being held for questioning. You had virtually no rights, you could-
n't make a phone call, and it went on your permanent record. Things
came to a head in the late '50s when a nurse was murdered near Children's
Hospital and the police hauled in 1,000 men during the weekend. All of
them were black and they were held under investigative arrest. The black
community was up in arms. The NAACP demanded that they stop this
unjust practice. That incident became the impetus for a drive to integrate
the police force, which at the time had virtually no blacks or integrated
scout car crews. It was a trying time for the department. Many officers called
in sick rather than have to work with a black officer. Others just quit.

When I joined the department, the entire country was going through
rapid changes. The civil rights movement was sweeping the land.
President Kennedy had been assassinated in 1963, as was Medgar Evers.
Malcolm X was killed in 1965. Riots were breaking out in city after city
and Detroit was waiting its turn. The Vietnam War was starting to tear the
country apart and the drug culture was spreading. Detroit was heavily
segregated, with the far east side and far west side being almost entirely

white. Since children went to the schools closest to their homes, the schools were segregated as well. Mayor Jerome Cavanagh owed his election largely to the blacks, who voted heavily in his favor, believing he was fair and would integrate city services, the police department, and other areas. This integration was desperately needed.

I've always felt that it's a police officer's job to be fair and to enforce the laws equally. This was reinforced during our training. We attended a series of classes about equal justice, racial equality, police brutality, and how important it was for police officers to make sure we treated everybody fairly.

During a break in one of these classes, I was talking to a fellow recruit, who grumbled, "Isn't this a bunch of bull?"

I couldn't have disagreed more, since I thought what they were saying was absolutely true.

"That's just liberal bull they're feeding us," he continued, not paying the least bit of attention to whom he was talking. "Trying to make you think you've got to treat people all the same."

"Listen," I said. "What they're saying is true: You *should* treat everybody that way."

"Come on," he replied. "You know there are some people you just can't treat that way. Some people are just assholes and you have to treat them like assholes."

This was during the second or third week in the academy, and I thought to myself, "What kind of an officer is this person going to be?" Luckily, he quit the department within a year.

Just as luckily, I made some great friends in the academy. Jess Davis, Howard Allen, Gilbert Stocker (who was later killed in the line of duty), and I carpooled to the academy together. Frank Mitchell—with whom I rode for my in-service training—and his family remain close friends to this day. In-service training was a part of our last few weeks in the academy. On Friday and Saturday nights we would go out in the field and work with seasoned officers for four hours, getting our first on-the-job experience. It was my first week out when I met Frank. I was assigned to the 2nd Precinct. Frank and his partner, Ed Stroker, were going to show me the ropes.

Sitting in the back of their two-man scout car, I was a very happy man. For the first time veteran officers were treating me as a fellow officer, teaching me about the job, speaking to me, and accepting me as one of their own. Suddenly a call for help came over the radio, "Wabash and Buchanan. Officer in trouble." When a police officer puts out a call for help everyone drops whatever he or she is doing and responds. Fast. After all, the next time it might be you that needs help.

It was a cruiser that put out the call—if four officers needed assistance you knew something was up. We sped to the location and found there was a big fight in full swing in the middle of the street.

"Okay, Ike, this is your first one," Frank said as we jumped out and got in the middle of it, finally calming everyone down and getting it under control.

"Well, what do you think?" he asked when we climbed back in the car.

I looked at him and smiled. "I think I'm going to like this job. Not the fighting, mind you, but yes, I'm going to like this."

Back at the academy on Monday we had to critique what we'd done that weekend. When I told everyone about the big fight, the other recruits were jealous. Everyone wanted to experience the rush of a good battle, and I'd had one.

It didn't take long to find out that not everyone in the department was colorblind like Frank. My second in-service assignment was at the old 16th Precinct, which is now the 8th. It's near the border of Detroit and the city of Redford. When I reported to the desk sergeant he told me to sit down and wait. I waited. And I waited. After thirty minutes two officers came out and looked at me, "We got one to go." I knew that the phrase "one to go" meant you had a prisoner to take to jail. It turned out they meant it a little differently—I was going to be the prisoner.

For the next three and a half hours I sat in the back seat of the car while we drove around, neither of them saying a word to me. Not a one. I later found out there was only one other black officer assigned to the 16th Precinct. I was starting to see that the department might not be everything my idealistic spirit had hoped it would be.

~

Upon graduation from the academy, I was assigned to the 2nd Precinct, which was where Frank Mitchell and Ed Stroker were. I couldn't have been happier. Being one of the most racially mixed, and busy, precincts in the city, they assigned four of the seven black graduates there. The first night, October 22, 1965, I was taken up to the locker room, which is where we kept our clothes. They were having roll call right down the hall in the squad room. The moment I walked in, the atmosphere turned chilly. No one would look me in the eye. In fact, they all moved to the other side of the room.

I recognized a guy there whom I had gone to high school with. He was trying to avoid making eye contact with me. We'd been pals for at least the last two years of school until he went into the Marines and I joined the Air Force. I walked up and said hello. He shook my hand, then disappeared, looking like he wanted to dig a hole and hide in it. I stood in that room with twenty-some-odd officers on my first night on the job and nobody spoke to me. Not a single person came up and said hi or hello, not a darn thing.

I remember standing in that room feeling very isolated and thinking. I was thinking about growing up, thinking about everything my father had gone through, thinking about Rotation Slim. I remembered all of the good things my father had told me about life. I remembered standing on that tarmac in Vietnam and saying, "This is going to be hell, but I'm going to make it."

Little did I know that I had just entered hell.

Two sergeants walked into the squad room yelling, "Roll call! Roll call!" Everyone lined up, very military-like. We were in full uniform and we were standing at attention. The sergeant called names in pairs, and assigned us to our cars.

"Smith."

"Here, sir!"

"Peterson."

"Here, sir!"

"You're assigned to Scout 21."

On it went until he called out -------. I'll never forget that name, but out of respect for his family, I'll call him Jackson.

"Here, sir!" the officer said.

"McKinnon."

"Here, sir!" I shouted proudly.

Then in a very loud voice Jackson spat out, "Jesus Christ!"

I froze. Everyone laughed, including the sergeants. The laughter was so loud I didn't even hear what car I had been assigned to.

After roll call I took my ticket book, my teletypes—which we were supposed to read and be briefed upon—the small notebook every officer carries, and my flashlight and went downstairs. As I looked around, I could see that every scout car but one had two officers in it, so I walked over to that car and said, "Excuse me, am I working with you?"

Nothing. He didn't even look at me, just stared straight ahead.

I asked him again, but he wouldn't say a thing, so I walked back into the station. "Sarge," I said. "I don't know who I'm working with. I don't remember the officer's name, could you help me?"

He took me outside and pointed to the officer I'd just spoken to. I climbed into the car and sat next to this man, and I swear he didn't say a word to me for the next eight hours. From midnight until 8:00 am we drove around the precinct and he didn't open his mouth. Not once. It got completely absurd. At about 4:00 am he pulled up to a restaurant called

Hygrades, at Michigan Avenue near 24th Street. It was where most of the
officers in the precinct ate. He got out of the car, walked into the restaurant, and went into the restroom. Then I watched him come out of the
restroom, sit at the counter, and order a meal!

I sat in the car laughing. "This is incredible!" I thought. "We have a
freakin' crazy person here!" Right then and there I decided that if this was
really so hard for him then I was just going to make it worse, because I was
going to stick with him. Being a police officer was what I wanted to do,
and dammit I was going to do it.

After he finished his leisurely meal we got our first call of the night: a
breaking and entering near Michigan and 20th. As we jumped out of the
car, he finally said his first words to me, "If anyone runs out of the house,
shoot him." Then he ran around to the back of the house. It hadn't mat-
tered to him if the guy was innocent, guilty, or just someone leaving at the
wrong moment, he wanted me to blow him away. Well, someone did run
out of the house and I grabbed him. It turned out to be a neighbor who
had stopped by to check things out because he had seen the burglar enter
the house. He was lucky I hadn't listened to my partner.

Things improved the next night, but not by much. I went out on
patrol with a different partner. This guy spoke to me. Once. He told me to
listen to the radio while he took a nap in the car. For seven and a half
hours we sat in an alley while he snored. I just knew we were going to get
caught, and this only my second night as a cop! At 7:30 am I woke him up
and he proceeded to chew me out royally for not doing my job. Apparently
I was supposed to wake him up earlier so there would be enough time to
ride around and put some mileage on the car to make it look like we'd
been driving around all night. So for the next half hour we drove back and
forth along the Lodge while he cursed me the entire time.

I've been asked if these first two dreadful nights shook my resolve at
all to continue to be a police officer. And my answer has always been quick
and honest—never. I can surely say that these first two nights only
prompted me further to stay in this system, and, in fact, to change it.
There was no looking back.

While there were many wonderful people in the department, there
were also a number of them who tried their damnedest to make things
very difficult for anyone who was different. Some officers placed a card-
board partition between them and their black partner; others used a
cleaning solution to wipe the steering wheel and the seat where the black
officer touched. There were even some who never spoke to us or even
acknowledged our presence, exhibiting a lack of respect for us as people
and fellow officers just because we were black. Oddly, many of those same
men would be wonderful with the black children on the street, playing

around with them and treating them with apparent dignity and respect. Then they'd turn around and not even acknowledge our existence in the station house. It was confusing, though I'm sure the problem was that they felt we were a threat to their job and livelihood. But I grew somewhat immune to it and didn't let it bother me. Anytime they'd do something to me I'd think about Rotation Slim. I'd step back, be objective, and go out into the community and do something positive, being energized by the number of people who appreciated and respected the job we were doing.

But sometimes it just got too ridiculous for words. There was a special detail called clean-up, where four of us—three whites and a black— would go into a bar. The black guy would go in and make a buy, then the others would raid the place. One Sunday night, Officer Rinke, who usually went out with us, had gotten the night off. A sergeant, whose name, ironically, was White, joined us. Ike Selick, one of the few Jewish officers at the time, was there as well. Yes, it was the Ike and Ike Show.

During our shift, we were all sitting at a table in Mr. Ren's Bar, across from the downtown post office. Sergeant White wouldn't say a word to me. He insisted on talking to me through one of the other officers. I looked directly at him and asked if I could have four hours of comp time. He turned to Ike Selick and asked, "What did he say?"

Ike, realizing what was happening, relayed the question.

"Oh, he wants four hours of comp time? Tell him it's okay," White said.

Ike turned to me, "He says you can have four hours of comp time."

"Tell him 'Thanks,'" I said, then got up and left.

It's amazing what some of us had to put up with. I hadn't been on the force long when a young black man by the name of Howard King was brought into the police station and then allegedly beaten by the police. A black officer, Ken Johnson, witnessed it and came forward, making a statement to his supervisor. He was completely ostracized for this, ultimately being transferred a number of times because no one wanted to work with him. He eventually took an inside job and became a lieutenant, but the Blue Curtain had taken its toll. The Blue Curtain says that you keep quiet about anything another officer might have done wrong, regardless of its severity. The odd part is that being black, Ken hadn't been accepted by the rank and file as a police officer until he said something, and once he did, they ostracized him. On top of that, Ken and the officer who was allegedly involved in the act of brutality were, and are, friends. And that officer is probably one of the nicest people around. There doesn't seem to be any animosity between the two of them. It was the misguided officers with their prejudices and their Blue Curtain that took it to an extreme and made Ken's life miserable.

Although I had a lot of conversations with Ken during this dark period, I didn't come forward to speak on his behalf. Ken chatted with a lot of the black officers, but in the end no one stepped forward. The Blue Curtain was indeed a powerful entity. It was a very disappointing time for everyone.

~

I had my own telling incidents in this area. Having gone through what I did with Rotation Slim, I wasn't about to let anyone do something like that to another person. If I saw an officer getting aggressive, I'd tell him to stop. He'd usually look at me like I was crazy, and ask what the hell my problem was and why I didn't support my partner.

"You need to know that if you do this, number one, I'm going to stop you. Number two, I'm going to go back and tell the supervisor that you did it. There's no reason to be doing this."

On any number of occasions I had officers ask me, "Are you going to back me or are you going to back this asshole?"

"Why are you calling this person an asshole?" I'd ask. "You're investigating him for something he *might* have done and you've already decided he's an asshole. Then you want me to condone your hitting him for no reason."

"We're the police and we've got to stick together."

Wrong answer. Sticking together doesn't mean letting someone do something that you know is wrong. It was especially galling since they didn't accept me as a police officer because I was black, yet they expected me to stand up for them regardless of their actions. Understand that this wasn't the norm within the department—the overwhelming majority of officers didn't think that way—but unfortunately there were plenty who did.

I never talked about these, or similar incidents, to my parents. They'd ask me how it was going, and I'd tell them things were going great. Occasionally, Jess Davis, Howard Allen, and I would get together and talk about it because we were all going through similar experiences in the department. But we all had the desire, the urge, the need to succeed as officers, and nothing was going to keep us from our dream. We had already made it through the process of getting into the academy, which for a black at that time was very difficult. All you needed was a couple of parking tickets or a moving violation, maybe poor credit, and it was grounds to keep you off the force. I had such a squeaky clean record that there wasn't much they could do. And luckily, I'd had Avery Jackson on my side, because there was one thing that almost kept me out. My depth perception. Or rather my lack of it.

When I took the department's eye exam I was told that I might not be able to join since I had a problem reading one of the eye charts. I went back to Avery and said, "Well, I guess I'm not going to make it."

When I told him why, he said that I should go see a private optometrist, Dr. Preston, who had an office on Brush Street. Apparently it wasn't uncommon for the department to use the slightest possible defect to discriminate against blacks. It also wasn't uncommon for people like Avery and Dr. Preston to know how to work around it.

"Here's what you do," the doctor instructed. "Look for the numbers that are truly illuminated, the ones that really stand out."

I went in and passed with flying colors.

∾

It didn't take long before I discovered another, even darker, side of the Blue Underbelly. One night an officer and I responded to a call about the burglary of a furniture store. I searched one part of the building while he searched another. I heard him yell, "Ike! Ike! Come here!"

I ran in to find him standing in front of an open safe with an incredible amount of cash lying there.

"Look at this," he said.

I'd never seen that much cash before.

"Here's what we're gonna do," he said. "You take half and I'll take half."

I was incredulous. "What the hell are you talking about?"

"I'm talking about splitting it fifty-fifty."

"No, no, no, no," I said. "We have to turn that money over."

"No way. This is some damn Jew's store and he'll pad the books to cover it anyway. You know how Jews are."

I said, "Wait a minute, man. We're police officers. We don't do that kind of stuff."

"So you're not going to take half of the money?"

"No, I'm not," I said. "And if you do I'm going to tell."

He couldn't believe his ears. "You are?"

"Yes, I am."

"Then I'll never speak to you again."

"Now that would be a great loss to me," I said sarcastically.

He left the money. What else could he do? I wouldn't stand for the dishonesty and I wasn't afraid of the consequences. It wasn't a year later that he ended up in Jackson Prison for taking money on the job. Imagine that.

∾

Jess and I started working as partners, which was the best thing that could have happened to us both. We were working in what was probably the most racially mixed precinct in the state, with a lot of white southern and Appalachian transplants living there, particularly in the area around 3700 Lincoln Street. One evening, Jess and I got a call about a domestic quarrel. We found a white man and woman in a heated argument on the porch. As we got out of the car they stopped their fighting long enough to yell, "No, no, no! We don't want you niggers!"

I couldn't help but laugh, because, honestly, I didn't believe it was actually happening. We decided to handle the situation in a professional manner.

"Well, which niggers *do* you want?" I asked the man.

"We don't want any, we want the real police. The white police."

"Oh, okay," we told him. "You two wait right here while we go get some of the real police, okay?"

As ridiculous as this was, it stopped the fighting. They had switched their focus to us, and, silly though our tactic may have seemed, it may have defused a very serious incident.

Jess and I made a pact that we'd spend time with the young people in the neighborhood. When I grew up, I always had my role models to look up to, but not all kids are that fortunate. I've always thought police officers should be good role models, but, as my early experience with Rotation Slim and my later ones as a new recruit showed, that's not always the case. The children in the community could sense that we were genuinely concerned about them—they'd freely talk to us, they'd listen to us. We tried to give them a positive, inspirational outlook, to help motivate and encourage them to seek a better life. We were, after all, two black police officers, which was rare enough at the time, but better yet we were two who worked together and were open to the community. We were honest with them, and when we had to be, we were firm. And since we *had been them* at one time, we could not only relate, but could understand their concerns.

Face it: Ethnic groups have their cultural differences. They have different ways of speaking, interacting, and relating to each other. Black people, for instance, have a long history of capping on somebody, or talking about their mother. It's not meant to be offensive, it's just the custom.

One summer day in 1966, Jess and I pulled a man over for speeding. He was doing forty-five in a twenty-five zone down West Warren Street on the near west side. He was a black man in his late forties, well dressed in green pants, a green shirt, brown shoes, and a straw hat. No sooner had we come to a stop than he jumped out of his car.

"Well, I'll be," he exclaimed. "It sure is a pleasure to see some colored officers out here."

"Well thank you, sir. Thank you," I replied.

"I'm telling you, I'd much rather be stopped by a colored officer than a white one."

Jess laughed as I thanked the man again. He knew what was happening—this guy was trying to run some game on us, hoping to get out of a ticket.

"Every time I get stopped by one of those white officers they treat me bad and they give me a ticket or take me to jail," he continued, not missing a beat. "But see, I know the colored officers won't do that."

He was doing such a good job of this that I decided to see how far he would take it.

"Sir, do you have a driver's license and registration?"

"Why yes. Of course I do, officer." He pulled his license from his wallet, all the while piling it on thicker and deeper. "You know, officer, I'm going to tell you. Yes, it's true. I mean it's so good to see some colored officers out here and you and your partner there are two very good guys."

"Well, thank you, sir," I repeated. "Now, do you have your registration?"

At this point, a small crowd had gathered. It was odd enough to see two black officers together, but to see them stop someone and have this absurd conversation was too much for them. I decided that it was time to call his bluff. I decided to pretend to write him a ticket. If he continued the effusive comments, I would let him off with a warning.

So I pulled my pen out and I pretended to write the ticket.

"What the hell are you doing?"

"Excuse me, sir?" I said, acting a little taken aback.

"What the hell are you doing? You're writing me a ticket, you no good big black bastard. You're just like those white police officers!"

Well, the game was over, so I wrote him a ticket. The people around him could hear this and they were getting a big kick out of it. I handed him the ticket.

"I got something to tell you, you no good black bastard," he went on. "Screw you!"

Without missing a beat, I said, "Yo mama."

The crowd started laughing, slapping hands and giving each other fives. The man busted up. See, back when I grew up, that was the ultimate putdown.

"You got me, you got me, you got me," he said as he shook my hand and walked away clutching the ticket. "I'm sorry."

I saw this man any number of times driving around after that, and every time he'd wave at me. We had established a rapport in our own way, on our own terms. And in the process, I established a rapport with the people in the crowd too. It let them see cops in a different light. So much so that it wasn't uncommon for people to stop us on the street and tip us off about something that was going down, because they felt we were all working for the same thing—the betterment of the city, the neighborhood, and the people who lived there.

~

One afternoon, Jess and I were on patrol when we received a call that a child had been struck by a car in southwest Detroit. We were driving Ford station wagons then. Since there weren't any EMS trucks yet, part of our job was to transport people to the hospital.

A large crowd had filled the street. At the center of it all was a young boy, unconscious, with his mother kneeling over him crying. She was a petite and very pretty lady who didn't speak English. One of the nuns from St. Anne's Catholic Church, which was right down the block, was talking to the mother in Spanish. It turned out that the boy, who was about five years old, had been struck by a car, and the driver was still on the scene. Our first concern was the boy, so we got the stretcher from the back of the wagon, put him on it carefully, and prepared to take him to Children's Hospital, which was about four miles away.

As we were putting the boy in the car, we were trying to tell the mother to come along. She didn't understand, so the nun translated. We agreed that it made sense for the nun to come along as well. So there we were in the car: Jess was driving, I was in the jump seat, and the mother and the nun were in the back with the boy. We were trying to get through the rush hour traffic as fast as we could, speeding up Vernor Street in that '67 Ford station wagon, with the siren blaring and the light on top flashing. Each time we'd get to an intersection I'd scream out "Right!" to let Jess know the coast was clear to proceed. As we started across Grand River Boulevard, a car cut right in front of us.

"You stupid son of a bitch!" Jess yelled at him. Then, remembering that we had a nun in the back seat, quickly apologized, "I'm sorry sister, I..."

"Don't be sorry," she said. "He is a stupid son of a bitch. Now let's get this boy to the hospital."

~

Maybe it's my affinity for children. Maybe it's just fate. But I feel very lucky to have been in the right place at the right time, over and over, to save a number of young lives. Over the years, I have received 22 citations and commendations—two of them departmental Life Saving Awards. One of the first was one of the most gratifying, proving that what goes around, comes around.

On February 24, 1966, I was working clean-up with Sergeant Harry Washington. Clean-up was when young black officers who hadn't been in the department long would spend Friday and Saturday nights working undercover raiding blind pigs, which were illegal gambling and drinking establishments. Harry and I were heading back to the station at about 3:00 am when I spotted a house on fire. As we pulled up, a young child ran to us, excitedly telling us that there were others still in the house. We crawled inside, keeping low to the ground to keep under the thickening smoke. We came across a young girl on the floor. We pulled her out of the house. There was smoke coming out of her mouth and nose. We pulled her mother to safety too. Unfortunately, we couldn't get to two other children, who died in the fire.

Harry and I were given citations for the rescue, but our biggest honor came years later. One day in 1974, I received a phone call from Belinda Solomon, the young girl we'd pulled from the fire. She thanked me for saving her life, and then asked if Harry and I would give her away at her upcoming wedding. It was one of the most thrilling and gratifying moments of my life, standing up at that wedding watching someone whose life I had saved continue on, happy and smiling.

A year or so later, in August of 1967, my partner L.C. Parker and I were on patrol at Bagley and Trumbull Street near Tiger Stadium when we saw a duplex on fire. We could hear children screaming inside. L.C. ran in one side and found his way through the smoke-filled stairway to the second floor, where he scooped up two children and carried them outside to safety. I went into the adjoining building, fighting my way through the thick smoke to find five children—the oldest being eight—and their teenage babysitter, all scared and crying. I led them out of the building.

As we stood out front, the babysitter told us there were two children still in a downstairs bedroom. We tried to get back in the building, but the heat and billowing smoke were too much. We broke a window trying to gain entry, but the flames shot out and pushed us back. There was nothing we could do—the two children died. L.C. and I received a departmental citation for the rescue. While it was nice to be recognized for what we did, there's no compensating for the lives that were lost. There never is.

Death is one of the most difficult things for me to deal with. I remember each and every situation. There's always a little bit of blame that you place on yourself and always a great deal of doubt. If you had been there sooner, things might have been different. If you had done something else, been in a different place, tried a little bit harder, things might have been different. You always question. It always stays with you.

CHAPTER *four*

The call woke me up at 5:30 am. "Ike, this is Sergeant Berryman. We need you at work right away. A riot just started."

"Sarge, you've got to be kidding," I said, and then hung up. This was either a bad dream or a bad joke. He called right back.

"Ike, I'm not kidding. This is for real."

I dressed quickly, jumped in my '65 black and green Mustang convertible, and made my way to the precinct. It was surreal. All along the way people were looting, just walking into stores and marching out with their arms loaded with food, clothing, just about anything they could get their hands on.

Three years previous, in 1964, a race riot had erupted in Harlem. Over the next several years, they had spread, hitting Cleveland, Chicago, Omaha, Watts, and Oakland. The department wasn't prepared, even though they knew it could happen in Detroit at any time. My initial involvement had been in June of 1966, when I was ordered downtown to the third floor, which is where most of the higher command officers worked—people like the chief and the superintendent—so I knew something was up. Once there, I learned that I was going to be teamed up with two men—a sergeant and another officer—to work undercover in the 10th Precinct, one of the busiest and toughest in the city. That was the area they figured was most likely to see a disturbance. The other officer was Tom Taylor, who had worked undercover for a long time, and the sergeant was none other than Bill Hart, who would later become the chief of police and figure prominently in the history of the department.

The three of us stationed ourselves in the area of Linwood, 12th

Street, and 14th Street trying to get a feel for what, if anything, was going to happen. The people were happy, almost festive. They were having a good time. We didn't sense that anything was wrong. Possibly the best thing that came out of it was that I got the opportunity to sit down and talk with two veteran black officers who had survived the department. It opened my eyes. And little did we know that one day two of us, Bill Hart and I, would each end up being the chief of police.

12th Street was known as a haven for prostitutes, having relocated there after Hastings Street was demolished. We rode around in an old green Packard with no air conditioning. The second night we were sitting in a vacant lot around Pingree and 12th just watching the throngs of people out for a walk, which was very common back then. We were just sitting in the car watching, waiting to see if anything was brewing. It looked like it was going to be a quiet, uneventful end to the shift.

Then a beautiful white and red Thunderbird convertible pulled up to the corner, with the top down, and a young, white, blond man in the driver's seat. "Look at what we've got here," Bill said. The man struck up a deal with a black prostitute, parked his car, put the top up, and, right there in plain sight of the entire neighborhood, took the money out of his wallet, put it in his pocket, and tossed the wallet in the trunk.

We all laughed. "Boy, this has got to be one stupid guy," Bill said.

The guy walked across the street and went upstairs. Within minutes, a group of young black men who had been watching this started taking his car apart. The guy must have heard the noise because he stuck his head out the window, saw what the men were doing to his car, and yelled, "You niggers better leave my car alone!"

Bill Hart looked at the two of us and said, "We better call for help. This guy's going to get himself killed!"

We radioed for backup and told them to send a cruiser, figuring that we might need the four extra men. The guy came hopping downstairs, pulling his pants on as he went along, still yelling at the young black men. Of course, they immediately challenged him, so he took off running north on 12th Street. The funny part was that we all had this stereotype in our minds of these fast-running black guys taking off after a slow-running white guy. But there you had at least ten young black men chasing this white guy down the middle of 12th Street and he's beating them flat out! I think they were more surprised than anyone! The cruiser caught up with him about a mile away and brought him back to his car. Needless to say, I think from then on he transacted his business deals at a different location.

~

The next summer brought more riots around the country. As the weather heated up, so did the civil disturbances. The first one hit Tampa. Then on July 12th, all hell broke loose in Newark, New Jersey. We watched it on television—the lootings, the burning buildings, the people dying. Mayor Cavanagh had set up hotlines, held meetings, and put together a Summer Task Force. He said he was "more fearful than at any time in the past five years of possible civil unrest." A lot of people didn't think it would happen here in Detroit. After all, the city was doing well, the economy was strong, and race relations seemed good.

July 22nd proved them wrong.

$\sim$

There was an eerie pall over the station house when I arrived that morning after having been awakened from a deep sleep. None of us had been through this before, since the last major riot had been in 1943, the year I was born, and I don't think there were many officers still on the force who had been there when it happened. We really didn't know what to expect. Sure, we'd seen and read about Watts and Newark, but to suddenly find yourself in the middle of it was a totally different experience. The truth was, none of us had been trained to deal with anything like it—not as police and not in the military. If it followed the pattern of the other riots that summer—and we had no reason to think it wouldn't—we knew that the first few days would have an almost festive atmosphere, but at some point it would turn violent.

The story went that the riot had started when a 10th Precinct cleanup squad went to close down a blind pig on 12th and Clairmont. A crowd of nearly two hundred gathered in the street when the police hauled off eighty-two people. Rumors spread through the crowd and the nearby neighborhood that there had been police brutality. As the last police car pulled away, someone threw a bottle at the car's rear window. Someone else threw a litter basket through a store window. The riot had begun.

No one knew if this was really true, but the way that summer was unfolding across the country, anything could have set it off. And if that hadn't, sooner or later something else would have. Even though Mayor Cavanagh was well thought of in the black community and had done a lot to help race relations in the city, there were individuals who wanted a riot to happen. They were waiting for it to happen, and would have ensured that one way or another, it would happen. And it did.

We were sent to the 10th Precinct, which is where I lived. It was the most dangerous and busy precinct in town, and most, if not all, of the looting and rioting took place there. It was a typical sunny summer day as we drove through the chaos to the 10th Precinct station house. We hadn't been given specific orders so we simply observed the events around us. The streets were filled with people carrying anything they could find. A white Cadillac convertible had its top down with a sofa sitting across the back seat. Two people lounged on it, each one holding a television set. As we drove by, they waved. It was insanely festive.

The station house was more like a madhouse. Officers were waiting for their assignments, and the Salvation Army had already set up a food stand to feed those of us who hadn't eaten. We were assigned to squads of three or four scout cars and sent out on patrol. Almost every business we drove by had its windows broken out, and people were piling inside to loot. We'd arrest a few, take them to the station, then head back out to catch some more. There were so many people looting that we had our choice of who we wanted to take in. We did this from 7:30 that morning until almost 2:00 am the next.

After the looting came the fires. They were everywhere. There weren't enough fire engines in the city to deal with it. We knew this spelled trouble—the fires were just the first phase of the violence. As we continued arresting people I could see the frustration growing, on their part and ours. We were on Linwood Street watching the looters running rampant when our sergeant had seven or eight of us line up across the street in formation.

"I want all you damned people to move away from here," the sergeant called out to the crowd.

"Go to hell, honky!" someone yelled back. It started to feel like a surrealistic Richard Pryor routine.

The sergeant took it personally. "What did you say?"

"I said 'Go to hell,' honky!"

So the sergeant broke ranks and took off after the guy. The crowd surrounded him and knocked him to the ground. We waded in to save him and finally got him back in the car. We got the hell out of there, fast.

Things were spiraling out of control. Not just the rioters, but the police too. I was driving home that first night with the top down on my car, still in uniform. As I crossed the overpass on the Lodge Freeway at Chicago, I was pulled over by two officers in an unmarked car. They could see that I was in uniform. In fact, they could see the insignia in my lapel that said I was with the 2nd Precinct. I opened the door and stepped out. One of the officers aimed his gun right at me. "You're going to die, nigger," he said.

It's true what they say about times like that. Everything went into slow motion. Through my heightened senses I could see this guy pulling the trigger, slowly, the hammer pulling back, the gun barrel aimed right at me. I dove into my car as the first shot rang out. As I peeled off in my Mustang he fired again. And again. It was like everyone was going crazy!

I never told this story to anyone until years later. I guess it was just too painful to bring up and made me feel more vulnerable than I cared to feel. Or maybe I thought it was a dream. You just don't believe that things like this could ever occur and, I guess, I preferred that it stay a dream. As he pulled the hammer of the gun back, there was a split second of total awareness when you have time to assess the entire situation. Why is this occurring? Why does he want to shoot me? How would this officer ever be able to explain what he had done? And the questions faded into one definite answer—I'm not going to die. It's not my time to go. And as I sped away and heard the storm of gunfire around me, I knew for sure that it was no dream.

Needless to say, I became extremely apprehensive—if these officers were doing this to me, what were they doing to people out on the street? There were 657 people injured and 43 killed during the Detroit riots that summer and I've always wondered how many of those were legitimate. How many had committed a crime? How many were randomly picked like I was? And how many died at the hands of overzealous officers like in the Algiers Motel incident?

This happened at the tail end of the riots, on July 26th, at the Algiers Motel on Woodward. Officers responded to a report of sniper fire, and before it was over three young black men who had been at the hotel with three white women were shot to death and seven other motel guests were beaten and abused. Three police officers and a private security guard were tried and found innocent. It was, and still is, very difficult to convict a police officer, especially when the issues involve race and there's a change of venue for the trial.

The Algiers Motel incident, perhaps more than anything else during the riots, divided the city. It divided the police. Many of us on the force, both black and white, knew that the games that were played in that motel weren't games humans played. It was racial, plain and simple. And there were also those who thought that the officers at the Algiers Motel hadn't done anything any officer wouldn't have done under those circumstances, that they played a game that got out of hand. No remorse—it just came with the territory. To this day, the Algiers Motel incident and the riots go hand in hand in most people's minds. The negative legacy and stereotype this caused for the Detroit police department lasted for a long, long time.

I was shocked at what had taken place. It was despicable. This was one of the darkest periods of my tenure on the force. It was a period when I was faced with so many questions. These were questions I never thought I would have to ask, and the answers were a source of shame and confusion.

CHAPTER *five*

The 1967 riots served as a wake-up call for both the city and the department. As the 1968 Kerner Commission report later declared, America was becoming "two societies, one white, one black—separate and unequal." The department realized that the community distrusted the police, much of the distrust stemming from the negative history of the force and from its lack of minorities—something some of us were aware of all along. The city hired an advertising agency, Campbell-Ewald, to put together a campaign aimed at recruiting minorities. As luck would have it, they chose me to be the poster boy. There I was, bigger than life, plastered on billboards all around the city. "There are never enough big men to go around," it read. Then we filmed a TV commercial on I-75 just as it was being built. It showed me—the big, black cop—saving a young white girl and her mother on the freeway. At the end of the commercial, the little girl was frightened and crying, so I reached down and wiped her little tears from her cheek. I don't know if it helped the recruitment effort—and it sure didn't get me a Hollywood movie contract—but it definitely helped my star within the department.

Thanks largely to this high-profile ad campaign and the publicity from the two house fire rescues I'd been involved in, I was approached by Lieutenant Ray Goode and Sergeant Bob Jackson about becoming the first black to join the Precinct Support Unit, a city-wide group that investigated most major crimes. I don't want to belittle the job any other officer does, but these officers were some of the hardest working, most dedicated people in the department. Guys like Jim Bardel, Jerry Malinkowicz, Freddy Arndt, and Bill Shine, who is still a close friend, taught me how to investigate. They were highly professional officers who weren't brutal to people, did their jobs as police officers, treated people with respect, and treated me as a fellow police officer. It was a great change and I felt very lucky to be there.

That's not to say everyone there was perfect. One day an officer shot and killed a man in the line of duty. I walked into the office and overheard him telling the other officers, "I shot me a nigger." When he saw me standing behind him he just turned and walked away. I stood there dumbfounded that he'd taken another man's life and could dehumanize him so. I told Bill Shine, who was a sergeant and a very rational person, because I was so upset. He said, "I understand, Ike. Wherever you go you're going to run into assholes. But you can't let someone's insensitivity get to you. As a man and a police officer, you should learn from this." And I did.

∼

On April 4th 1968, Dr. Martin Luther King was shot and killed in Memphis, Tennessee. The department went on full alert. Even though Dr. King preached nonviolence there was concern that we might see a repeat of the 1967 riots. Luckily, in Detroit some very cool heads prevailed and they spread the word that, since Dr. King was a man of peace, to be violent in his memory would be a travesty. Some American cities had violence anyway.

It was a very sad time for those of us who loved and respected him. Even though we knew his life had always been in jeopardy we never really thought anything like this would happen. I talked to people on the streets and emotions ran high. There was a feeling of utter disbelief and frustration, much like there had been when President Kennedy was assassinated. It was particularly touching and more personal to the people of Detroit, since it was here, at Cobo Hall in 1963, that Dr. King gave the original "I Have a Dream" speech. It was the shorter version that he gave later in Washington, D.C. that made the nation sit up and take notice.

We were on twelve-hour shifts patrolling the more tense parts of the city as a safety precaution. I was riding with one officer when he said, "You know Dr. King committed suicide, don't you?"

"What?"

"Yeah, he committed suicide."

"Wait a minute," I told him. "What the hell are you talking about?"

"He paid a guy to kill him so he could become a martyr."

"And where in the hell did you get that ridiculous story?"

"Everybody knows it. It's no secret that he was asking people to kill him."

"Wouldn't it be a better idea to die an old martyr than a young one?"

I said jokingly. But he wasn't kidding—he was dead serious. "I can't believe that the greatest civil rights leader in the world has just been assassinated and you're desecrating and demeaning his memory by saying such a ridiculous thing."

He shrugged his shoulders. "Well, that's just what I heard."

"Well, quit repeating it!"

Dr. King's death contributed to the feeling of hopelessness in the city. Here was a man people looked up to and put their faith in, cruelly taken from them in his prime. All the great men who were trying to help the masses were being snatched away. President Kennedy. Bobby Kennedy. Malcolm X. Martin Luther King. What was the use? Where was the hope for the future?

A couple of days later I had my answer.

I was riding in a car with three officers on the west side near Dexter and Richton. I was sitting in the rear right seat holding a sheet of paper that listed all the cars that had been stolen during the past twenty-four hours. As we drove, I was looking around and checking the sheet. I spotted a white Mustang.

"Stop! It's stolen!"

We screeched to a halt and I jumped out of the car. The driver of the Mustang knew we were onto him so he started to back up. As he did, a tall guy jumped out of the passenger side and took off running west on Richton with me in close pursuit. As we got down the block he darted into an apartment building with me right on his behind. He threw open the outer door, ran into the hall, and slammed into a door on the left. I practically ran right into him. I threw my left arm around his neck. Just then the apartment door opened and I saw five men standing there with automatic weapons aimed right at me—I'd stumbled into a meeting of some Black Panthers. I drew my gun, which was a Smith & Wesson .38, a peashooter compared to what they had.

"Don't move!" I said, my voice quivering two or three octaves higher than usual. I knew I was going to die. I just knew it. Images of officer Glen Smith, who was killed six months before at 16th Street and Myrtle, flashed through my mind. I could see my mother, crying, looking down at me as I lay in my casket. It's a horrible feeling when you think you're about to die.

I started backing out of the building, my arm around the guy's neck, repeating over and over, "Don't move. Don't move." One of the guys, who appeared to be the leader, could see that I was shaking. He kept saying, "Be cool, man. Be cool."

"I am cool. I am cool," I lied, shaking like a leaf.

We got out to the sidewalk. I was still holding the guy in front of me as a shield. I could see through the front window into the apartment—

their automatic weapons were still aimed at me. I kept thinking, "I know they're going to shoot, I'm going to go down, and I'm going to die, right here on the spot."

I looked around. Where the hell were my partners? I later found out that they'd chased the car and, since I hadn't had my small prep radio, they hadn't known where I was. I started backing down the street, my gun out, with the crook of my arm tight around the guy's neck, headed toward where I had left my partners. People started coming out of their houses and apartment buildings and walking toward me.

I heard a calming voice say, "Everything's gonna be okay, man," and before I knew what was happening, the people who had come out of their houses surrounded me, forming a circle around me and my prisoner, as I backed down the street, protecting us as we made our way back to Dexter and Richton. I thanked God for them. I wished I could have thanked each and every one of them personally for saving my life, for protecting me, for looking out for me, and for renewing my faith in humanity once again.

~

Not long after that, I was transferred to the Recruiting Section, which made sense since I had a pretty high profile thanks to that ad campaign. I had been there for only a brief time when I got a call from Sergeant Bill Shine.

"McKinnon?"

"Yes sir, Sarge."

"Don't call me 'Sir,'" he said.

"Okay, sir, I won't call you 'Sir.'"

"Dammit McKinnon, I said don't call me 'Sir'!"

I said, "Yes, sir."

"What are you doing?"

"Why, I'm talking to you on the phone."

"I mean what are you doing this afternoon?"

He wanted to meet me at five o'clock in the basement of the City-County Building at a restaurant called Greenfield's. He told me not to tell anyone.

"Yes, sir. I'll be there, sir."

"I told you not to call me 'Sir'!" he said, and slammed the phone down.

As I sat in Greenfield's waiting for Bill, I tried to figure out what this could be about. Bill walked in, sat down, and looked me straight in the eye.

"What I'm about to say will affect the rest of your career on the Detroit police department," he told me. I was grasping for possibilities. Thoughts were flying through my head. Did I do something wrong? Was he going to try to get me involved in something I shouldn't be doing? What?

"Mayor Cavanagh wants you to join his security staff."

"You're kidding me." I was serious when I said that. I knew that Bill had a dry sense of humor and I needed to be sure he wasn't pulling something on me.

"Ike," he said. " I don't kid."

"Yes sir, Sarge."

"Dammit, don't call me 'Sir'!"

He told me that come Monday morning my inspector was going to get a blue slip, which is a departmental transfer. Now this was Friday night, and he was telling me that I couldn't mention it to a soul.

"This is a great job," he told me, as if I hadn't known that. "You'll be working for the mayor of the City of Detroit. You'll be driving him around, you'll be interacting with him and his family, and you'll meet a lot of people who will have a major impact on your life." He looked at me. "I'm telling you, Ike, you're gonna love it. But be prepared. Your best buddies will cut your throat over something like this because they all want the job. Come Monday morning at 9:00 am some of them are going to stop speaking to you."

I knew that Bill Shine had once worked the mayor's detail, but I never thought I'd get the opportunity. "Why me?" I asked.

"I've watched you for quite a while now. I like the way you carry yourself. You're a hardworking guy, you keep your nose clean, you're intelligent, and you're articulate."

"Keep it up, Sarge," I said, loving every second of it.

"Screw you," he replied with a laugh.

I was floating on air when I left the City-County Building. Here I was, about to be working for the mayor as a part of his security team. I went home, sat my parents down, and told them the news. Needless to say, they were ecstatic.

"Lord Jesus, my boy's gonna be workin' for the mayor," my mother said, with tears rolling down her cheeks. My father, who would talk properly almost as a counterpoint to my mother's southernisms, said, "Yes sir, I always knew my son would amount to something." Somehow we managed to keep the news to ourselves all weekend.

Monday morning I was in the office pretending to go about my business when the interdepartmental mail came in.

"McKinnon!" the inspector bellowed. Everybody looked up. "Get your ass in here!"

Everyone looked at me, wondering what I must have done.

"Who the hell do you know downtown?" he demanded.

"Sir, I don't know what you're talking about."

"That's bull," he said, waving the blue slip. "You've got a tit someplace downtown." His voice was getting louder. People outside his office could hear every word. "You gotta know someone downtown 'cause they got your ass transferred to the mayor's office. Go ahead and get out of here. But I swear you know somebody."

The truth was that I didn't. But thanks to Bill's warning I'd been prepared for the reaction. And there I was, listening to the first person who found out—a veteran black officer—show his true colors.

"Damn you," he went on. "You took my job, McKinnon. I've got more time on the job than you do. That should be me going down there."

He wasn't the only one. The other black officer in recruiting asked me who was pulling strings for me. No "Congratulations." No "We're proud of you." Just "Who do you know?" Only two officers offered their good wishes— one who had recruited and trained me, Rob Schick, and Alex Garanzini.

~

Working in the mayor's office gave me a more cosmopolitan perspective on life and on the spirit of the city. For the first time, I was exposed to business people, politicians, blacks, and whites working together to make a change in our community. Mayor Jerome P. Cavanagh was a brilliant, outgoing, handsome man who had all the earmarks of heading toward the Senate, possibly even the presidency. He pushed me hard and I thank him for it.

My schedule was to work on Tuesdays and Saturdays, each being a twenty-four-hour shift. The mayor was in the process of separating from his wife and had eight children who stayed with him most weekends. Every Saturday night he'd cook dinner for them. Here was this man, the mayor of the city, puttering around the kitchen cooking for his kids while I sat there and talked with him. He'd tell me about his life and ask me about mine. He encouraged me to go to college. He was an attorney, very involved in the civil rights movement, who was trying hard to make a difference. And so were his friends and associates. They were very strong, very dedicated people. It was an entirely different atmosphere than what I was used to in the department. There were no overt signs of racism. People were helpful and interested, and it was most gratifying.

When we were assigned to the mayor's security detail we were told to protect him but weren't given any special training. The mayor's office was on the 11th floor of the City-County Building and everyone knew it. Irate citizens would show up regularly. One day a very large man showed up and in a loud voice demanded to see the mayor. My partner, Sergeant Terry Driscoll, and I could usually finesse people out of the office, but this guy was yelling and screaming, adamant about seeing the mayor. The mayor happened to be out of the building, but we knew he'd return any minute.

"I want to see the mayor now!" the guy screamed.

I was talking to him, trying to calm him down, casually walking him down the hall toward the elevators without him even realizing it. He was pretty much under control by the time we reached the elevators. Suddenly, the doors opened and who should be standing there but Mayor Cavanagh.

"Mayor, I want to see you!" the guy yelled.

"Move!" I told the mayor, who by now was trotting down the hall with his security officer by his side. The big guy took off running after him, so I jumped on his back. Only it didn't slow him down a lick—he was running after the mayor carrying me with him! Finally Terry showed up and together we wrestled the guy to the floor, handcuffed him, and took him down to the 1st Precinct. There wasn't really anything we could charge him with, but at least we got him away from the mayor. They released him. Later that night he killed someone in a local neighborhood.

$\sim$

When Mayor Cavanagh announced that instead of seeking another term he would return to private practice, it set city politics in motion. Judge Roman Gribbs ran against Richard Austin, a black accountant who was the county auditor, chairman of the Wayne Country Board of Supervisors, and the first black to run for mayor. He was well liked and a good man, but Detroit wasn't ready to elect a black mayor. Gribbs, who was a very decent and honorable man, won the election. I stayed on as part of his executive security team and forged a great relationship with him and his family.

Needless to say, everyone was curious about the inner workings of the mayor's office. Two friends of mine, who were young students who had worked for the Urban Corps, had been begging me to let them see the office. So one day, when the mayor was out of town, I brought Martina O'Sullivan, a close friend who later made me her daughter's godfather, and Carol Martin, who's now a national TV reporter, into the inner sanctum. They were a bit awed by the big desk, the view of the Detroit River, and, of course, just the fact that it was the mayor's office.

There was a back door leading into the office that the mayor used when he wanted to avoid coming in through the lobby and front door. No one—but no one—other than the mayor and his security detail ever used it. Well, I was playing the big shot showing Carol and Tina the office, getting so bold that I sat in the mayor's chair and put my feet up on his desk. Suddenly, I heard a key being inserted into the lock of the back door. I can't even imagine the look that was on my face as I leaped up and started running out of the office in a panic, leaving Tina and Carol standing there. It would have been my ass if I had gotten caught in the mayor's chair!

"Gotcha!" my partner Terry Driscoll called out as he strode in through the back door, the key in his hand, laughing as loud as he could. I had to wait for my heart to stop pounding before I could join them in the laughter.

~

When I left the mayor's security detail, it was to work in the Public Information Office, which was one of the most exciting and educational times of my career. I worked the midnight shift with Fred Williams, who was my sergeant. Our job was to report the night's police events to the media. Unfortunately, that was usually crime and violence, because Detroit had been pegged as the "Murder Capital of the World" and the media was keyed in to the negative. Unfortunately, this still tends to be true. I wish we had done more to relay the good things the police were doing, but that was not the way it happened. I liked talking on television, but I particularly enjoyed radio. I have to admit it—I've always been a ham.

Working the midnight shift was never easy. Either it was hectic and you didn't get a break or it was quiet and there was a tendency to, well, fall asleep. One night, I was working by myself and, since I'd been studying hard for my college finals, I was exhausted. I knew that I had about an hour before another TV or radio station would call, so I shut off the lights and stretched out on the desk. Being a light sleeper, I knew that I'd wake up if anyone approached. Suddenly, the lights switched on, I bolted upright, and standing in front of me was none other than the tough-talking, no-nonsense field duty officer, Inspector Joe Areeda.

"What the hell do you think you're doing?" he demanded.

"I'm resting my eyes, sir."

"Bullshit! You were sleeping." I could see my career and my life slipping away right before my sleepy eyes. "Well, wake up and talk to me, dammit. And don't do it again." We sat there and talked for three hours, and trust me, I never tried that again.

One night, though, Fred just couldn't help himself. We were having a particularly rough shift and were completely bushed. Every hour, the press would call and we'd tape something with them. When radio station CKLW called, Fred insisted on going on live. As he spoke, I could see his head nodding. When the reporter asked him the next question I could hear Fred snoring loud and clear—live on the air.

∼

On March 29, 1969, a group called the Republic of New Africa held a convention at the New Bethel Baptist Church on Linwood. Driving by, Patrolmen Michael Czapski and Richard Worobec saw a black man standing out front holding a rifle. When Czapski got out of his car to investigate the man opened fire. Czapski died instantly. Worobec was shot in the leg and back, and managed to crawl to his police car to radio for help. Within ten minutes, police surrounded the church, stormed inside, and arrested everyone—142 people.

Like the Algiers Motel incident and the riots, the New Bethel shooting divided the city. A local television reporter fanned the flames by playing the officer's radio call for help over and over. Many people were outraged that the police would violate the sanctuary of a church and arrest people. Others thought that when Judge Crockett ordered the immediate release of thirty-nine people who had been arrested it condemned the department's action. Still others called the release an outrage. Many people fled the city, both blacks and whites. No one was ever convicted of Czapski's murder.

At about this same time, Police Commissioner John Nichols assembled a special police unit to help staunch the rise in street crime called Stop The Robberies, Enjoy Safe Streets, which went by the acronym STRESS. The thirty or forty members of this unit hit the streets as decoys, walking around acting drugged, with money hanging out of their pockets, hoping to become robbery targets. Most of the officers were white. Most of the robbers were black. Amazingly, there was a sudden increase in the number of young black men being shot and killed in the progress of a robbery. The stage was set for what may have been the most explosive, politically charged, and divisive police issue in the history of Detroit.

CHAPTER *six*

Inspector Richard Boutin, the commanding officer in charge of Public Information, recognized a pattern emerging: Almost weekly there was a shooting involving the STRESS unit and a young black male. Boutin was relentless as he again went to Commissioner John Nichols and told him what he was seeing. He explained that if he saw it, sooner or later others would too and then the department would have a major problem on its hands. The commissioner was a very tough, hard-nosed man and he backed his men without hesitation. Even though the writing was on the wall, he decided not to take any action.

As the pattern continued, we kept sending our reports to the commissioner. Others picked up on it too, and they were starting to protest. One part of the community defended what was happening, saying it was a deterrent to others who might consider going out and robbing people. After all, the argument went, it was only criminals who were being shot, right? Ken Cockrel and Sheila Murphy (who would later become Sheila Cockrel) were among those who were loudly anti-STRESS. Ken was an electrifying speaker. He was a tall, thin, handsome attorney who exuded charisma and wasn't afraid to challenge the power elite and say what was on his mind. He and Sheila, along with brilliant attorney Justin Ravitz, galvanized the community to fight STRESS.

Their following grew with each young black man who was shot. More and more people demanded that STRESS be disbanded. They protested to the city council, they protested to the police department, they protested just about anywhere they could find an audience. They pointed out that New York City's STRESS unit worked well and was highly effective, but not Detroit's. Here it was largely unsupervised and out of control. On March 9, 1972, it broke wide open.

~

I was on duty in the Public Information Office when the call came in that a STRESS squad had conducted a midnight raid on a house at 3210 Rochester Street that they suspected of being a center of illegal gambling. I called Inspector Dick Boutin and woke him up.

"This is Ike. There's been a shooting over on Rochester Street."

"Okay."

"It involved some Detroit police officers and Wayne county sheriffs."

"Okay."

"They shot at each other, sir."

He hung up.

I called him once more and convinced him that it was true. He came right in and we spent a long night with the media, all of us in disbelief. It turned out that the supposed illegal gambling house was in fact a Wayne County deputy sheriff's apartment and a gun battle had ensued between the STRESS officers and members of the sheriff's department. In the end, one deputy had died and two had been wounded, resulting in a major rift between the Detroit police department and the Wayne County sheriff's office.

This was all the city and the department needed. It was right on the heels of two highly publicized shootouts between the Detroit police and a small group of self-professed revolutionaries who claimed to be fighting drug trafficking in the city. John Boyd, Mark Bethune, and Hayward Brown shot at four undercover officers who had stopped their car, then three weeks later killed patrolman Robert Bradford and wounded his partner. This set off an intense manhunt for the "mad dog killers," as Commissioner Nichols dubbed the men. The manhunt got so out of control that some officers were going house to house, kicking doors down and barging into homes looking for Boyd, Bethune, and Brown. This event divided the community even further—one side almost salivating at the prospect of a lynching, and the other claiming that it was racially motivated because the police only seemed to react like this to crimes committed by black people. Brown was arrested after firebombing a birth control clinic at Wayne State University. It was said that the attack on the clinic was done as a diversion, but Brown's actions were always a mystery. You never really knew what to believe. Boyd and Bethune were killed in shootouts in Atlanta. Brown was convicted of the firebombing, but was acquitted of all charges relating to the murder; his lawyers painted him as a drug fighter who was trying to clean up the city. He became a local folk hero for standing up to the establishment and the police department and for not stopping his quest to rid the community of drugs, which he claimed were being brought in and protected by the police.

~

In 1972, I was promoted to sergeant and transferred to the 10th Precinct, where I got to work with a number of veteran sergeants who had years of experience and were eager to teach, particularly Sergeants Roland Raska and Dick Kratz. There was never a dull moment.

Early one morning I was on patrol with my driver during the midnight shift when we heard over the radio that there was a chase in progress in the 2nd Precinct heading north on 12th Street, which meant they were coming our way.

"Let's get over there," I said. "They might make it into our precinct and need assistance."

I had a hunch of how this chase would end—the same way most of them do, with someone getting his behind kicked, and I wanted to make certain none of my officers got involved. Chases bring out the adrenaline in you. It's a very primal experience, and all it takes is a little resistance or one too many smart words and oftentimes control is lost. It becomes a mob mentality. If someone has forced an officer to endanger his life, then somehow the officer feels justified in penalizing the offender with some degree of police brutality. It doesn't happen in every instance, but in far too many. The longer the chase, the higher the probability of a brutal act. The officers feel as if they can justify their actions, so as a result you have very few men who will try to keep it from happening. They lose all sense of self-control.

The chase was getting closer, heading straight toward us. The closer they got, the more I could feel my own adrenaline flowing. I knew this was happening to the other officers, and I hoped against hope that I could be there when the chase ended to help make sure that it turned out peaceably.

The vehicle went out of control on LaSalle Boulevard near Central High School, a block from where we were. It was 2:00 am. The streets were wet. As we turned the corner, I saw something I just couldn't believe, the type of thing that I'd heard about but never witnessed. To this day I hope I never see it again.

The scout cars were parked in a circle with their headlights on. In the center, bathed in a pool of light, were three people on the ground being kicked and beaten by the officers. As my patrol car screeched to a halt I jumped out. "Stop it, goddammit! Stop!" I shouted, running over to an officer who was kicking who I later discovered to be a fourteen-year-old boy. I grabbed him by the shoulder, swung him around, and ripped the badge off his shirt. He took off running toward his car. I snatched another officer's gun from his holster and he ran as well. The rest of them jumped into their cars, turned off their lights, and peeled off into the darkness. I managed to grab a third officer, hold onto him and eventually pass him off to one of my men, Atwood Stevenson, with whom I had graduated from the police academy. My blood was boiling. This made absolutely no sense to me; someone could have been killed. On the way back to the precinct house, I looked at my driver and asked him what he'd seen back there.

"Uh, sir, the light was blinding me. I didn't see anything," he lied. I knew what was happening—the Blue Curtain was drawing closed.

"You cowardly ass," I said, trying to contain myself. "You know what we both saw and now you're afraid to admit it." For whatever reason, he resigned from the department a little while later without ever making a statement about what he observed.

By the time I got back to the station, the officers involved had already contacted their supervisors, who had gotten hold of mine. He was there waiting for me. The word was out that this crazy black sergeant had stopped some officers from doing their job, interfering when they were dealing with men who had forced them to risk their lives.

"Ike, come in here," the lieutenant said, the minute I stepped into the precinct. As soon as the door to my supervisor's room was closed, he turned and asked me what the problem was.

"Lieutenant, the problem is that a number of officers were savagely beating three young men on the street and I stopped it."

"What are you going to put in your report?" he asked.

"Exactly what I saw."

"Ike," he said. "If you do that you're going to cause these guys to lose their jobs."

I looked at him in amazement. "Lieutenant, I'm not causing anyone to lose their jobs. If they lose their jobs, it will be because of what they did back there." I wasn't about to let the blame fall on me for stopping something I knew was wrong.

He eyed me carefully. "Are you sure you want to do that?"

"I'm as sure as I can be."

It wasn't long before the lieutenant from the 2nd Precinct showed up, and he went through the same routine. I refused to budge. He gave me the same argument—that they were going to lose their jobs if I reported the truth. He was pissed. I was upset. I didn't know who all of the officers involved were, but I had a badge, a gun, and an officer in custody.

A little while later, I was sitting in the office typing up my report when the phone rang. It was my inspector, who had been having a nice quiet night at home.

"How are you doing, Ike?" he asked, being cordial.

"I'm doing fine, Inspector." I repeated the story, telling him what I saw and that I was going to report it.

"Ike, you know you're going to cause these guys to lose their jobs, don't you?" I was getting tired of this line of reasoning, especially since my viewpoint wasn't getting through to him any more than it had to the others. "I have to tell you," he continued, "the people in the department aren't going to look on this favorably."

"Which people is that, sir?" I asked. "Look. I'm a sergeant, and my job is to supervise. I'm supposed to make sure people do their jobs fairly. I'm supposed to make sure people don't commit these kinds of acts. And that's what I'm doing."

"Okay," he said angrily. "Do what you've got to do." Then he hung up on me.

When I walked out of the office, I could see the reaction of the officers in the precinct. All of them, black and white alike, were upset at me because I was going against their Blue Curtain. If stares could be as venomous as they looked when I walked through the station, I would have been dead on the spot.

I went into the interrogation room to see the boys who had been beaten. It turned out they were two brothers and a cousin. They appeared to be okay, so I got their phone numbers so I could call their parents and have them picked up.

"What the hell do you want?" the brothers' mother said gruffly.

"Ma'am, your sons have been beaten up by the police and they're here at the precinct station."

"Screw 'em," she said. "They deserve to get their asses whipped. You tell them to get their little asses home." I couldn't believe this. I was catching hell from every direction. "I don't give a damn about them," she said as she hung up.

Here I was with a case of police brutality over which I'd alienated everyone at two precincts, and I didn't have a witness. To top it off, the boys' mother couldn't care less. She wasn't going to come get them, much less press charges. I had to figure out a way out of this mess I'd gotten myself into.

After I took the boys to a relative's house—their mother didn't care if she ever saw them again or not—I returned to the station to find all the officers who had been involved in the incident waiting. I brought them in and, with my boss there, read them the riot act. I told them how disappointed I was in them and how it was terrible for them to do things like that. I went on and on, knowing full well that I had no one to back me up, that there was no mother to press charges, and that there was really noth-ing I could do. But they didn't know that.

"Sir," one of the men said. "I know I can lose my job for this, but I promise you that I'll never get involved in something like this again. I've promised your boss that if you take it easy on me, I'll never do it again."

"Never again," I said. "I want you to understand this. Never."

The three of them shook my hand, and then embraced each other. It was probably for the better that it turned out the way it did, because it set the tone that I wasn't going to take any crap from anyone, and that if I saw it I was going to report it. It certainly didn't hurt that I came out of it looking rather benevolent.

Eight months later I transferred to Internal Affairs.

CHAPTER *seven*

The political atmosphere in the city was ripe for upheaval. Mayor Gribbs decided not to run for reelection. Coleman Alexander Young, the long-time black state senator, put his hat into the ring, as did John Nichols, the white police commissioner, who, not surprisingly, had the support of the police force. In a city that was forty-four percent black, this was the first time there was a strong possibility that a black mayor could be elected.

The major campaign issues were crime and STRESS. Twenty people had died in confrontations with STRESS officers, seventeen of them black. Coleman Young went so far as to promise to abolish the group, saying "We want professionals, not Keystone Kops."

Coleman Young won the election by 16,000 votes, only four percent of the 415,000 that had been cast. As promised, one of the first things he did was disband STRESS. Within the department, many people were extremely upset and vocal, because not only was a black man now running the city, but they felt that an effective crime-fighting tool was being taken away. Meanwhile the black community felt pride and exaltation about Young's election, and nothing but gratitude over his disassembling STRESS. The surrounding communities, on the other hand, had their own reason to be upset, and it had nothing to do with STRESS. In his inaugural speech at Ford Auditorium, Mayor Young declared that "Drug dealers, pimps, prostitutes...should hit Eight Mile," which in the black community was common slang for "get out of town." Unfortunately, those who lived past Eight Mile Road, which meant predominantly white suburbs, didn't know that, and it caused a firestorm—they thought he was aiming to send the criminals out their way! He spent the first days of his term defending the comment—which I loved—but it reinforced just how polarized the people of the Detroit area were.

It would have been nice to think that the election meant that people's attitudes had changed, but that just wasn't the case. The very day after the election, I was sitting at my desk in Internal Affairs with my partner, Jim Humphrey. The room held ten or twelve sergeants, and at the time I was the only black officer assigned there. I overheard one of the sergeants say, "Now that we have Coleman Young as mayor, when we do our reports we'll have to put more *yah sirs* and *dat der* and *dis here* in them." I couldn't believe what I was hearing. I felt like I was in a very bad dream and wanted to shake myself, pinch myself, wake myself up. I honestly thought we had moved past this.

He kept it up, saying that we'd have to "fill our reports with *mo fos* and *sho nuffs* 'cause dat's how dey talk."

Jim grabbed my arm as I stood up, but I shook it off. "What the hell are you talking about?" I demanded. "Why are you saying this crap?"

He looked at me. "I'm not talking about you, Ike. I'm talking about the rest of those people."

"The rest of those people could be my mother, my father, and my friends who might just speak that way." I was livid. I was prepared to go to battle. I started walking toward him and Jim stood up, saying, "Ike, if you fight, I fight." I was walking toward the sergeant with every intention of a physical confrontation when the lieutenant walked into the room. He didn't know what had happened but he could tell something was wrong.

"Is everything okay?"

I stopped in mid-step, took a deep breath, and walked back to my desk. I gathered my things and left the office with Jim at my side. I was absolutely furious. Here we had a man in the Internal Affairs Section of the Detroit police department who was supposed to be just—but how could you say those things and be considered fair?

Jim apologized for the guy, saying that he was just an ignorant asshole. "You don't have to apologize for him," I said, still steaming. I got calls at home that evening from others in the unit who also apologized, saying that those kinds of things shouldn't happen. I thought about Rotation Slim. I thought about all the things that happened when I was a young officer and wondered if it would ever stop.

Later that night, my commanding officer called and asked me to come to his office the next morning.

"Ike," he said when I sat down. "I thought when we talked about your being transferred here you said you could handle this kind of stuff."

"What do you mean?"

"You know, stuff like what happened yesterday. I hear you overreacted to some kidding."

"Obviously, you have the wrong story," I told him, trying to be calm. "Before you go any further why don't you talk to Jim Humphrey, Norbert Kozlowski, and Stan May, who were there. They can tell you exactly what happened and maybe that will change your mind." I walked out of the room.

He must have talked to them because he called me in later and apologized. I said, "You don't need to apologize for what this guy did. What you should look at is what you said to me without hearing what I had to say."

He apologized for that, and then asked, "What do you want me to do?"

"I'm not the one in charge," I told him. "You're going to have to make that decision. But I want you to think about this: You have a situation here where a person who works in the so-called elite Internal Affairs Section has made some very strong, disparaging racial comments about people in the community he serves. Think about that."

He ended up transferring the sergeant who made the remarks out of the unit, which spoke volumes about the man that he was. Needless to say, there were some officers who stopped speaking to me because they thought I had done something wrong. After all, the sergeant *was* only kidding.

∾

Coleman Young brought affirmative action to the city of Detroit. The first place it was implemented was the police department, which was predominantly white male, with very few blacks, women, Hispanics, and other minorities. It was a noble idea to try to level the playing field and the mayor wasted no time putting it into place.

The original policy was to promote white males and black males one for one. This kept the black males happy, but angered the white ones who would have been next in line for promotion. It pitted officer against officer, causing arguments in the precinct stations and even resulting in a physical confrontation outside the Federal Building. When the mayor expanded the program to include black women it upset some of the black male candidates because it diluted their chance for promotion. It wasn't long before the white female officers protested that there weren't enough of them being promoted. Before long the order was: one black male, one white male, one black female, one white female.

At this point, just about everyone was upset. Historically, the most eligible person on the list had been promoted. When affirmative action was first instituted, an officer could possibly have to wait one turn while someone else was promoted ahead of him. Then it became three, then four. Add to that charter promotions, which allowed the chief to promote whomever he wanted out of order, and there was no way of having any idea when it would be your turn. The police union was strongly against affirmative action, backing the majority of its members who were white. This caused the black members to get up in arms, because the union was using their dues to fight against their promotions. As if this weren't enough turmoil, the administration started sending women out on patrol for the first time, which, while a wonderful idea, caused concern among some male officers, and especially their wives, who just knew what would happen if men and women worked together all night! Some families were broken up by it, but I'm not sure if it was a problem specific to the Detroit police department.

It was chaos with so many points of upheaval.

Realistically speaking, most whites felt affirmative action interfered with their future, their career, and their family, taking money from their pockets and food from their kids' mouths. The blacks said it was about time, since that was what had been happening to them for hundreds of years. I firmly believe that a great number of the problems the department faces today—from recruiting to quality of service—are directly attributable to the advent of affirmative action and how it was implemented. So many officers have lost their commitment to the city and the department, feeling as if they've been abandoned. Their prevailing thought was, "To hell with it. We might as well bide our time until retirement since they've taken away what was rightfully ours."

At the same time, many of those elevated to positions of authority within the department didn't possess many of the requisite managerial skills necessary to effectively run the department. But because they'd been in the right place at the right time, or thanks to political considerations, many were thrust into command positions. Who you knew became increasingly more important, and it was flaunted. It was common knowledge for those wishing to advance that soliciting assistance from sources outside the department could help them move up the ladder. It was quite unsettling. I'd been taught that to remain objective you had to keep politics out of police work, but the department felt like a huge, never-ending game of political football, with police careers determined by political considerations and favors owed.

Advancing within the department had always been somewhat political. Buying tickets to political functions was now the most important step to getting promoted. Over the years, as a matter of principal, I was adamantly against purchasing tickets to political functions, even though it was evident that those advancing were doing so. A number of rising stars not only bought tickets, but sold them on duty, pushing hard and working their way up the ladder in the process, regardless of the fact that more competent, harder working, educated officers, both black and white, were being passed over and not considered. It was one of those things that was unspoken, but widely known. Even Chief Hart, a nice man who was always fair and treated me with respect and dignity, once told me, "Ike, you should buy a ticket to the mayor's function." That was it. Plain and simple. I finally capitulated and purchased a ticket. Guess what? Within months, I was promoted to inspector. I felt as if I had gone against everything I believed in. Were the most qualified people, regardless of race, really getting the promotions?

The climate in the department became increasingly hostile and divisive. Officers who had studied long and hard and scored well on the promotional exams were finding themselves low on the promotion list, and they resented it. Their rationale was, "I didn't do anything to black people. I didn't enslave them. Yet I'm being penalized for what my forefathers might have done." They studied, they worked hard, and they placed well, but they found themselves being passed over.

On the other side were the minorities who said, "Because of a racist society and institutional racism my forefathers never had the opportunity to prepare as you have. They never had equal opportunity. All we are trying to do now is level the playing field." These are both very strong arguments. No matter how you looked at it, it offended and angered someone.

Mayor Young was the driving force, catching the brunt of this because he was the one who championed affirmative action. There was a story that he was riding in his limo down Jefferson when a white police officer directing traffic by the Renaissance Center gave him the finger. They said that he was transferred that same day. It didn't help that the mayor never attended police functions like graduations or funerals, or went to the hospital to see an injured officer. Police officers are a very clannish group, and we like to feel like someone cares. It didn't seem like Mayor Young did.

∾

One night, I was sitting at my desk in Internal Affairs when I received a call from my former partner, Sergeant Dick Kratz, who was still assigned to the 10th Precinct.

"Hey, how you doing?" I asked.

"I'm doing good, but I'm not sure how you're gonna be doing after I give you this information."

He had my attention. Especially since I knew he worked clean-up, which meant he had his ear to the bars because he handled minor drug busts. "What's up?" I asked.

"I have an informant who told me she was in Coleman Young's Barbecue Bar on Livernois near Chalfonte," he explained. "She's worked with me before so I kind of know her. She says she was at the bar with a friend and they made a buy from a relative of Mayor Young."

I sucked in a breath. "Man, you're kidding."

He was serious. Here I was, new to Internal Affairs, and this major allegation was dropped in my lap. Most people think Internal Affairs only looks into police corruption, but they're also in charge of investigating anything relating to city officials. I got what little information he had, wrote it up, and turned it in to my supervisor, Dan McKane, who was the inspector in charge of Internal Affairs.

At the time, I didn't know that there had already been a long history of investigations into Coleman Young. I was just being a good sergeant, passing along the information I'd been given. McKane's response was pretty much the same as mine.

"What do you think?" he asked, once he got over the initial shock. "You think it's true?"

I told him that, as far as I knew, Sergeant Kratz was an honest guy and he obviously trusted me, because he came to me with the information. I left the office and went back to work, figuring I'd done my duty. Two days later I got the call—I was in charge of the investigation.

"Wait a minute now. Me? I'm a young sergeant," I told McKane and George Bennett, who was the deputy chief. Bennett was a tough, no-nonsense man who had successfully investigated corruption among narcotics officers in the 10th Precinct. He was a very secretive person, so much so that in practically every conversation he spoke in almost a whisper. He'd been one of my training sergeants at the police academy when I joined the department, so we were acquainted, but with the large spread in rank—he was a deputy chief and I was a sergeant—we weren't exactly close.

"You'll work the investigation, you'll work it by yourself, and I'll make sure you get anything you need," he told me. Yes, I was in charge of the investigation. In fact, I was the only one who would be working on it. That way it would be kept quiet and self-contained. I was to go and cultivate sources, trying to find out if there was any truth to this allegation. In hindsight, I think they were very conscious of the fact that they were sending a black officer out to be the sacrificial lamb. If a white officer had led the investigation, Young would have screamed racism when he found out. But as I said, this is in hindsight.

McKane and Bennett assured me that the three of us would be the only ones in the department who knew about the investigation and that I had no reason to doubt anyone's honesty. Little did I know what was happening behind the scenes.

∾

At the time, I wasn't sure why they had given it to me—a fairly inexperienced investigator in the unit—but I figured that, since I was the only black in the unit, they thought I'd have a better chance of getting people to talk. In addition, I was relatively new, meaning that I was probably clean and honest. Besides, I already knew about it.

I wasn't sure how to start, so I met with Kratz, and then with the informant. She was very convincing. She said she'd been in the bar when her friend bought dope from the mayor's brother-in-law.

"What are you getting out of this?" I asked her.

Not surprisingly, she wasn't doing this out of a feeling of civic duty or a sudden need to become an upstanding citizen—she was being squeezed. This is how we got a lot of our information. You pick someone up and before you know it they're doing what we used to call "Singing like the Temptations." And let me tell you, she was singing all five parts!

I put a body microphone on her before she met with her friend. During the course of the conversation, the friend verified what I'd been told. I tried to get the informant to set up a meeting between her and the mayor's brother-in-law, but he wouldn't bite. Over the next few weeks, I spent a great deal of time in the back of an undercover van at Livernois and Chalfonte taking pictures of people coming and going from the bar. I'd run the license plates so I could keep tabs on who these people were. And while I wasn't having in-depth conversations with my inspector, I was turning in all of my reports.

One day, I was approached by Lieutenant Bill Hoston, a tall, distinguished veteran, who took me aside and said, "I understand that no one's supposed to know what you're working on, but let me tell you this: Make sure you cover your behind. There are people who know about your investigation and they'll use you. They'll do anything they can to turn things around and make it look like you're the one doing something wrong. If I were you, I'd get someone to back me up."

I looked at him, troubled by what he was saying, the reality of the situation starting to sink in.

"Don't trust everybody who's around you," he continued. "I'm telling you, cover your behind."

I thought back to the previous week when I'd left my apartment and noticed a car following me. I did a quick loop and got behind him, but whoever it was jumped on the freeway and took off. I didn't get his license plate number, but it happened twice.

What Hoston told me scared the hell out of me. I literally ran to the Drug Enforcement Agency. I went in cold, not knowing a soul there, and met with Ron Depottey and another agent, whose name, ironically, was Ray MacKinnon. I told them what I knew. They listened intently, then thanked me for coming in and suggested that we work together. The four of us went to the FBI and met with Agent Randy Prilliman. I didn't tell anybody in the department that I'd done this, not even my supervisors. I had no idea what was going on or whom I could trust at that point.

I continued to spend part of my time sitting in the van taking pictures and the rest on the streets listening. Nothing was really developing, except maybe the curiosity of the other officers in Internal Affairs, who were wondering what I was doing on a case by myself. I kept Ron Depottey updated, and somewhere along the way he and the FBI decided they could trust me and started to share information. As the case evolved, it turned out that what I was involved in was just a piece of a much bigger puzzle. And Kenny Garrett was a big part of that puzzle.

$$\sim$$

Oddly, there were two drug dealers in Detroit named Kenny Garrett. Black Kenny Garrett ran dope on one side of town, while white Kenny Garrett worked the Cass Corridor. The white Kenny Garrett was the one they said had ties to the mayor's brother-in-law, operating out of a number of bars in the Cass Corridor, including Sabb's Bar and the Golden Ducat. The department had a deep undercover investigation into the Garrett organization. Garrett suspected that two men he was selling drugs to were officers but he couldn't verify this, so he was desperately seeking information. He was allegedly paying some Detroit police officers to tip him off about who was working undercover and what they were doing.

The department finally assigned another officer to help me out, someone from undercover narcotics named Bernard Taylor, or B.T. He had great contacts and knew about narcotics. I knew about investigating. It was a good combination.

I quickly learned more about Kenny Garrett and what was going on in the police department, largely from the prostitutes in the Cass Corridor, many of whom took to talking to me, probably because they appreciated having someone who would listen to them honestly and openly as people, not as prostitutes. They'd call and share their lives with me, telling me everything, including which officers were using their services. One woman, who went by the name of Dootsy, had been a hooker for years. She'd call me from a pay phone and tell me about Kenny Garrett and what he was doing. She'd tell me about which officers were on the take, and which ones I needed to watch out for. My eyes were being opened to an incredible web of lawlessness on the part of many Detroit officers. I had to believe it since so many different sources were corroborating it.

One night I went into a bar undercover pretending to want to hook up with a prostitute who was Dootsy's sister so I could get some information she had for me. I was wearing a body mic, and another officer, Curtis Burton, was monitoring it from outside in the car. I went into the Golden Ducat and a pretty young blonde, who hadn't been in the business long, sat next to me. It didn't take her long to proposition me.

"Look, I'm not in here for business," I said. "I'm here to meet somebody." She ignored me and started rubbing my thigh. "I told you, I'm not in here for business," I said, but she kept grabbing at me anyway. "Hey, I'm a cop."

She looked at me like I had just dropped in from Mars. "So, cops do this kind of business too."

~

A joint decision was made to raid Kenny Garrett's drug markets, which stretched through the Cass Corridor, as well as his house in Sterling Heights. The FBI, DEA, and Detroit narcotics division coordinated the raiding parties. Everyone involved met in a room at the Federal Building at 11:00 am to be briefed on the who, what, when, where, and how of the roundup. Needless to say, these things have to be done with the tightest security—the slightest leak can blow the whole operation. That's why once everyone's in the room no one leaves until it's time to roll.

We were all briefed, had our assignments, and were ready to hit the street, only we had to wait. The search warrants needed to be signed by U.S. Attorney General John Mitchell, who was in Congress testifying. So we waited. And waited. Finally, they released us for lunch and told us to come back in an hour. B.T. and I looked at each other—you just didn't do that!

When we got back to the Federal Building, the warrants had been signed, so we headed out. One after another, the raiding parties were coming up dry. Each place they went to was a location we *knew* was the center of drug activities, yet they were as clean as a church! It was so bad that when we drove up to Kenny Garrett's house he was sitting in his car out front waiting for us.

"Hey guys," he said, like the cocky person he was, "I've been waiting on ya. What took you so long?"

This convinced me even more that whatever was going on there was bigger than me, bigger than the DEA, even bigger than the FBI—though I still didn't know who or what was involved. Years later, information came to light, through the Freedom of Information Act, that someone close to the mayor had been an informant for the FBI. But it ran deeper than that. I'd been warned to be careful and to watch my back. I'd had a high-ranking person in the department offer me a job working for him, then in the middle of the conversation casually ask me how the investigation was coming—the secret investigation that, at the time, only three people in the department were supposed to have known about. Obviously, it had been no secret. How many more knew, or were possibly involved?

Later we busted Kenny Garrett on outstanding charges. After he was sentenced to prison, my new partner, Norbert Koslowski, and I went to visit him at Michigan Federal Prison in Milan. I was wearing a hidden microphone in the hope that he'd tell us about some of the officers we'd heard he was paying off.

"I know you, McKinnon," he said to me. "Everybody talks about you. They all knew you were investigating them."

"So what do you have to tell us?" I asked.

"Well guys, I'll tell you this," he said, leaning forward. "Thanks for the nice visit. That's it. I know a lot, but face it, I don't want to lose my life."

Kenny's brother Ronnie, on the other hand, wasn't so bright. He talked a lot, passing along good information. It didn't take long after he was arrested and sent to a federal prison in the Midwest for him to be killed.

I kept plodding along, but things were leading nowhere. It had turned into a game of cat and mouse, and I was having more and more trouble finding the mice. One time, we were staking out a bar when a man we had followed the previous week walked up to the car, looked in at us, and waved. Somehow they were more aware of what we were doing than we were of what they were doing. Our original informant disappeared. We never found out what happened to her, but I can only guess. The investigation was dead-ending quickly.

This widespread corruption within the department was something that frightened me tremendously at this time, and it didn't appear to be getting any better. The longer I stayed in Internal Affairs, the more cynical I was becoming. I convinced myself, though, to stay upbeat during this wave of pessimism, and I did. To be honest, there were times when I felt like leaving, but then I'd remind myself of my own priorities—to serve the community and do the best job that I could. I had to rise above the rest of the officers who were capable of being corrupted. But when given the opportunity to leave Internal Affairs, I left without giving it a second thought.

~

In the midst of the investigation, I'd taken my promotional exam for lieutenant and had finished in the top twenty, gaining the rank of lieutenant. Bill Hart, who would later become chief, was the deputy chief in charge of Headquarters Bureau. We'd always had a good relationship and he asked me to work for him. "Wherever you want me," I told him. I became the head of the Sex Crime Unit.

With that, my involvement in the investigation stopped, and from all appearances so did the investigation. No one was arrested, it was never made public, and most important, there was nothing found to implicate Mayor Young. But that didn't mean that he wasn't upset about it.

After I'd been transferred to the Sex Crimes Unit, Executive Deputy Chief James Bannon—who was the number two man in the department and the requisite white "counterbalance" to Chief Hart—took me on as kind of a protégé, often sending me out to give presentations and make speeches when he couldn't attend. One day he told me about a discussion he'd had with the mayor, who was upset that I hadn't told him about the investigation while it was going on.

"Who the hell is doing this investigation?" he demanded of Bannon. When told that I was the investigator, he wanted to know what kind of guy I was. Bannon said that I was a straightlaced, honest guy. The mayor was flabbergasted. "Why in the hell didn't that nigger come to me and tell me about it?"

"What did he expect me to do?" I asked Bannon. "I'm a sergeant. I find out about something that's going on and..."

"Ike," he said. "The mayor figured that being a black officer you should have come to him and told him about it."

"I'm sorry, but that's not the way I do business. It wouldn't be ethical."

No, it wouldn't. But it would have been politics as usual.

CHAPTER *eight*

I was still working at Internal Affairs the day I walked into the lobby of the Veteran's Memorial Building, which is where our offices were, and saw a vision: a beautiful woman with an incredible smile standing there waiting for the elevator. I didn't know if she worked in the building or not, but over the next few days I started seeing her around more and more. I knew that I wanted to meet her. What I didn't know was that she would end up becoming my wife.

I'm not a very forward person when it comes to things like this. Besides, I'm black and she's white and you never know how a prospective date might feel about interracial dating. I went to visit a female friend who worked in the building, Aletha Risker, whom I had met while I was a bodyguard for Mayors Cavanagh and Gribbs. It turned out that the young woman I saw was Patrice Bauer and she worked in the same office as Aletha. Before I could say a word, Aletha smiled and asked, "You want to meet her?"

"No! No! Wait!"

This, of course, was her cue to get on the intercom and page Patrice to her office, all the while with me mouthing, "Don't do this! Please!"

A few minutes later, Pat walked in and Aletha introduced us. She was smiling and I was tongue-tied. We talked for a few minutes. "I was going to ask Aletha to join me at my favorite restaurant, the Clamshop on East Grand Boulevard, right after work. Why don't you join us?"

She did. We had dinner and a great conversation. I was trying to think of a way to see Pat again, so I told them that I was also a karate instructor and invited them to join the class. I'd studied Korean style karate for a number of years with Ken Johnson and Mr. Kim at the Tang Soo Do

School and after achieving my first-degree black belt I started teaching. To my surprise they said they'd do it!

Aletha asked Pat to give me her home phone number so I could call and let her know when the class started. She did, so that evening, when I got home, I called and asked her out. She told me later that she knew all along what I was up to. To this day, Pat continues to tell everyone about our first date, which at my suggestion was the movie "Detroit 9000," one of the first films shot on location in the city. They used hundreds of local extras in the movie, including yours truly, who appeared on the big screen for all of five seconds. Believe it or not, I made her sit through it twice. From that night on we have been inseparable.

∾

I knew that Pat's race was a potential problem for some: In 1973 interracial couples were still rather taboo. One person in the department had told me to "stop dating that white woman or your career's gonna be shot," but I didn't care. I've always been open and honest and this was no exception.

My mother fell in love with Pat the first time I brought her home. My father waited until he and I were away from everyone else, and then looked at me very solemnly. "Sonny," he said. "You know that woman's white, don't you?"

I said, "Pop! You're kidding!"

"Nope. That woman's white. I just wanted to let you know."

You could always count on him.

He asked me if I was sure about Pat and, when I said yes, he took her right into the family, falling in love with her too.

In early 1975, we decided to get married. At the same time that we were planning the wedding, I was preparing for the lieutenant's exam. I scored high—number nineteen on the list—but due to affirmative action it was hard to tell when I'd actually get my promotion. We set a wedding date of October 18th, with a honeymoon in Tahiti to begin the next day.

There were people in the department who advised me not to go on the honeymoon. What if they started a promotional class while I was gone and I missed it? It could be years before there were any more promotions in the department. I figured that this was our honeymoon, we'd made plans to go to Tahiti, and we were going regardless of the consequences. I had studied hard for the exam, and I had done well. If I didn't get promoted this time around, I knew I would the next time. Besides, I had an ace in the hole.

I knew Chief of Police Philip Tannian from my days on Mayor Gribbs's security staff. He was considered an outsider, having come to the department from the FBI. This, in itself, led some people in the department to dislike him. But he was a smart man and we got along well. I'd never asked anyone for this kind of a favor before, but I really wanted to know what he could tell me about the promotion situation.

I went to see him and he greeted me warmly. We made small talk, then I told him about my impending marriage and my concern about a possible promotional class starting while I was gone.

"Congratulations on your marriage," he said. "When is it that you'll be returning from your honeymoon?"

"November 4th or 5th," I said.

He looked at me and smiled. "The class will start on November 6th."

We had a beautiful wedding in the PIME Mission's San Francesco Chapel, which is a gorgeous church on Oakland Boulevard in the heart of Detroit, then went to Tahiti for two wonderful weeks.

~

Pat was raised in Detroit and graduated from Wayne State University. When I met her, she was working for the city in the Employment and Training Department, but she soon transferred to the Budget Department, where she honed her money management skills. She left to work at the Detroit Institute of Arts as an administrator and, in 1991, was appointed as the budget director for Wayne County.

Surprisingly, we've had virtually no problems stemming from our interracial marriage. None that were blatant anyway. We've always taken the position that if someone does have a problem with it, it's their problem, not ours. We live in a diverse downtown neighborhood that includes a wide cross-section of people. We've traveled throughout the world and have yet to run into a problem, even in the South. Of course, we've experienced the occasional stare. And I'm sure that there were people who disapproved, but they wisely kept it to themselves.

We did get used to, and were sometimes amused by, the look of surprise on people's faces. I attended the FBI Academy in Quantico, Virginia for three months to be part of a class of executive level law enforcement people from all over the world. Out of 250 attendees, perhaps four were black. Even though we spent a lot of time together, we really didn't know anything about each other's families. Pat flew in to attend the graduation ceremony, and when she and I walked in together you could see the jaws drop.

Years later, when I became chief, and our lives became very public, many people were surprised to see me on television with my wife and two interracial children. About the only time I can remember it being an issue while I was chief was when a local black talk radio station hostess decided to make one morning's discussion topic, "Ike McKinnon and His White Wife." The amazing thing is that Pat has such a short drive to work that she very seldom listens to the radio in the morning, yet for some reason she did that day. She called me at the office, livid, and ranting about people's twisted attitudes. I told her the best way to handle the situation was to use that handy switch on the radio and turn it off.

~

Our first son, Jeffrey Christopher McKinnon, was born on March 4, 1978, a few months after my mother passed away. I always felt that God took one person away and gave us another to take her place.

I was always squeamish about childbirth. You always hear stories about cops bringing babies into the world in the back seat of the police car, but not me! When I was a rookie, I responded to a maternity run at the north end of the 2nd Precinct. As we walked in the house, the woman was screaming, "The baby's coming! The baby's coming!" My partner, Jess Davis, and I got the stretcher from our wagon, put her on it, and carried her out to the car. I sat in the back with her and all the way to the hospital she kept yelling, "The baby's coming! The baby's coming!"

"Not on my watch it isn't," I told her. "You just keep your legs crossed. The baby can't come until we get to the hospital. I don't care what you do, keep your legs crossed!"

So it wasn't surprising when I told Pat that I didn't want to be in the delivery room when Jeffrey was born. She wasn't hearing any of it. "You were there when he was created, you're going to be there when he's born." Enough said.

We crawled into bed and Pat leaned over to kiss me goodnight. Suddenly she got this strange look on her face and said, "I think my water just broke." Since the baby wasn't due for another month, I asked, "Can you fix it?" It was an incredibly short labor—Jeff was born in Hutzel Hospital an hour later. And yes, thanks to my training during two Lamaze classes I not only witnessed his birth, but this proud dad bravely cut the umbilical cord.

Being the first son, of course, he was special. He's always been the spitting image of me but with lighter skin. He's straightlaced, conservative, very focused, and a great athlete.

Our second son, Jason, was born April 24, 1984. His birth was an adventure, and life with Jay has been that way ever since. I was in charge of the Tactical Services Section at the time. I took Pat to her ob-gyn for a checkup, since all signs were pointing to another early delivery. The doctor said that she was beginning to dilate but not to worry. "Go home and relax. The baby will be here next month."

No sooner had we walked in the front door of the house than Pat groaned. "I think it's a contraction." We rushed to Hutzel Hospital, where the doctor told us Pat was going to give birth that day, and, if I wanted to see the baby born, I'd better change into some scrubs fast. I ran out, found some scrubs, and changed as fast as I could. But when I got back into the room Pat was gone!

"Where's my wife?" I asked a woman who was cleaning the room. She looked at me puzzled. "My wife! Where is she?!"

"Oh, you mean the white lady who was in here?"

"Yes, that wife."

She pointed toward the delivery room, so I made a mad dash down the hall, skidding to a halt when I saw Pat through the window. Our doctor hadn't had time to get there, so I was a stranger to the doctor in the delivery room. No sooner had I walked in than he told me to get out until I had a surgical mask on. I ran back into the hall and looked around, trying to figure out where I could get one. I spotted a nurse walking by, snatched the mask from her face, turned it inside out, and headed back into the delivery room to hear the doctor telling Pat to push. Right then and there Jason was born. As I grabbed my wife's hand and bent down to kiss her, I insisted that the baby's middle name be Patrick, in honor of his mom and the hectic delivery she went through.

~

Jason's a wonderful son. He's a dreamer with an incredible attitude and an imaginative sense of humor. He's a great writer and probably will be a standup comedian someday. You couldn't ask for two better children.

Our children never had any problems with their mixed heritage. It's perfectly natural to them, just as it is to us. They learned about my family's heritage as well as Pat's. They went to private schools because we wanted them to have the small classes, the attention, and the nurturing that would help them to do well. Also, it was a more diverse atmosphere, which would better prepare them for the real world. Unfortunately, our society is largely segregated and the world isn't; we wanted them to be prepared. We took them everywhere with us—to dinner, to the theater, to concerts, on vacation, wherever. Children should be exposed to as much as possible as they're growing up—to take it all in, to absorb the world around them, and to learn how to act in public.

Just as I learned from people in the community when I was growing up—most notably from Mr. Bunche and Mr. Hughes—so did Jeffrey and

Jason. Earl Van Dyke, who was the musical director for Motown, was our neighbor. This man, who was a great musician and had traveled around the world working with more famous people than I can imagine, would spend hours talking with Jeffrey about Motown, about music, and about life. Once Jeffrey had to write a paper for school about someone he admired, and he wrote it about Earl. He presented the paper at the main library in Detroit and it won an award. Earl was so impressed by this that, even though he was very ill at the time, he came to the presentation and stood up to be introduced to the audience. This is the kind of person who makes a difference in people's lives.

When Jeff was graduating from Grosse Pointe Academy his class chose me to be their commencement speaker. I was honored. Since it was a small class of about twenty-six, I was able to say something personal about each child, mentioning their unique talent or their aspirations. Years later, when Jason was graduating, his class also asked me to speak. It was like going home. It was a true honor to speak at my children's graduations. I like to think that they enjoyed it too.

CHAPTER *nine*

After the inconclusive ending to the investigation of Coleman Young's brother-in-law, I was looking forward to my new assignment as lieutenant in charge of the Sex Crime Unit. I knew it would be interesting and rewarding, but didn't anticipate how depressing it could be at the same time. The first thing I saw as I stepped off the elevator on the seventh floor of police headquarters was a row of wooden chairs lining the hall. This was where the rape victims would sit, right out in public, hurt and demoralized, becoming further victimized just knowing that every person who walked by knew what had happened to them. It disturbed me greatly that they had no privacy and no way to maintain their dignity.

Audrey Martini was a sergeant there. She was a very intelligent, progressive person who by all rights should have been in charge of the unit. She'd written most of the training manuals and was, in fact, doing most of the training. I utilized her vast knowledge and experience to learn how to run the unit.

We talked about moving the waiting area in the hall and she suggested a back room that was used for file storage. Like most police work areas, the Sex Crime Unit was an open room full of desks where everyone could see everyone else. Some nights there might be four or five rape victims sitting in the hall with two or three suspects being interviewed at different desks around the room, all out in the open. There was no semblance of privacy or dignity for the victims.

I had the file cabinets moved from the back area, then had it enclosed. That gave us a private waiting area where victims and their families could stay, away from prying eyes. I thought it was the humane thing to do and most of the officers in the unit thought it was great. But my deputy chief was livid. He demanded to know how I dared to do something like this without letting him know. He took me to task and made me justify my action. The department was male-centric, extremely chauvinistic, and obviously my deputy chief's hurt ego was more important than the women who had been raped. His resistance to change was symbolic of the "why do you care?" mindset of the department, and, more specifically, of some of the supervisors, and I was outraged.

≈

Working in the Sex Crime Unit affected me deeply. In all the years of being a street officer and a supervisor, I thought I'd seen it all, but here, for the first time, I was witness to a person's complete inhumanity to another person. People don't understand the incredible savagery of rape, of how dehumanizing it is. It really opened my eyes to the way men think about and treat women.

It's been said before, and it's true: Rape isn't about sex, it's about power. It's about a man making a woman completely subservient to him. I can't count the number of rape victims that I spoke to while I was there, learning firsthand how it affected and ruined their lives forever. I remember talking with a woman who had been raped forty years earlier and she still remembered it as if it had happened that day.

I made it my goal to educate people about the reality and tragedy of rape. I quickly discovered that a great number of people didn't want to listen or pretended that it wasn't a problem. They preferred to keep it out of their minds, to pretend it was not there, and to push it aside as if it were not a problem. They didn't want to get involved. That's the tragedy about crime prevention: If people would get just a little more involved it would make a tremendous difference. If we were able to get 20,000 or 30,000 people to volunteer to help out in the city for Devil's Night or Operation Clean Sweep, why couldn't we get those same people to mobilize to protect our children, our families, or any victim of crime? It just doesn't seem to happen. I certainly wasn't the only one in the unit to preach this, but I took it upon myself to bring the issue of rape to the public. I talked to groups and gave presentations throughout the city and around the state. It was great being able to do something that might effect a change and have an impact on the crime rate.

Any rape is a bad rape, but some were just horrific. One case that affected me profoundly was that of a young woman who was kidnapped and held for five days by a group of men. During that time, she was kept on a dog chain, fed dog food, beaten, raped, and tortured. It was beyond anything that most could ever have imagined. Somehow she escaped while they were out of the house, breaking free and running out of the house naked, and was taken in by an older man who called the police. Another time, three men kidnapped a Canadian woman when her car broke down on the Lodge Freeway and held her for days, raping her repeatedly. In the public's eye, it was a racial incident, but the truth was that it was a horribly barbaric crime against a woman. How could crimes like this not stir one's passion to do whatever possible to stop such crimes from happening again?

Statistics tell us that only one of every ten rapes or sex crimes is reported to the police. Thus, when there were 1,425 rapes or attempted rapes reported when I took over the unit in 1975, in reality there could have been as many as 12,825 that we didn't know about. This is crazy! Violent crime is never justifiable, but it's especially abhorrent when you look at the long-term effects of sex crimes against women and children. Too many people don't seem to comprehend this—often because they still view women and children as second-class citizens.

～

Being so specialized, the Sex Crime Unit was often called in to assist on cases outside our jurisdiction. Over a period of several years, a number of children had been abducted in Oakland County, a suburban area just north of Detroit. They were held, molested, then had their lifeless bodies dumped where they could be found. This resulted in what may have been the largest murder investigation ever in Michigan. Virtually every law enforcement agency was called in to help, including the State Police. I became involved, publicly asking for leads that might help, as well as offering public education and safety awareness training. On one occasion, I was speaking at a community meeting in Ferndale, Michigan when a woman came up to me afterward and introduced herself. She was the mother of one of the children who had been murdered and she thanked me for helping raise public awareness of the problem and teaching prevention. Moments like that can be overwhelming.

They never caught the person responsible for those murders. You feel for the victims, but also for their families.

Another difficult area was pedophilia. Late one evening, I received a call from a film developing company in California saying they had some very disturbing photographs of a Detroit man having sex acts with children. They sent me the photographs, along with the information on the person who had mailed the film in for processing. The man was named Daniel Droney. It was absolutely heart-wrenching. The pictures showed

Droney in a variety of sexual poses with a number of young children. Here we were, seasoned cops who thought we'd seen it all, yet none of us were prepared for what we were encountering. These were extremely young children that he was with! We were shocked, appalled, outraged. We got a warrant from the Wayne County Prosecutor's office and went to search Droney's house. The living room walls were covered with giant enlargements of him with the children.

The people of the neighborhood were in shock when the news broke. Droney was a clean-cut, well liked, and well respected member of the community. He was in the military reserve and gave the neighborhood children rides on the back of his motorcycle, took them for airplane rides, even babysat for many of them. No one had any inkling of what he'd been up to.

We arrested him and brought him to headquarters, bringing the photographs along as evidence. A number of police officers who lived in Droney's neighborhood came to the Sex Crime Unit so they could look at the photos and make sure none of their children had been involved. I hated to do it, but I had to put a stop to it. I could just imagine an officer finding a photograph of his son or daughter with Droney, pulling his gun in blind rage, and blowing the guy away.

This was my first exposure to the sordid world of pedophilia and child pornography, but far from the last. My education continued when Brian Flanigan, a friend and reporter for the *Michigan Chronicle*—and later the *Detroit Free Press*—introduced me to an informant he dubbed "the Basketball Swish." He was a 6'7" pedophile who had no problem turning in other pedophiles. He loved thinking he was an undercover cop, helping us out by wearing wires and going into places we couldn't. He helped us put away a lot of people. I learned an awful lot from him, including a lot of information I could very well have lived without.

While sex crimes are a very serious matter, any job will have its share of lighter moments. One time a woman had been kidnapped at gunpoint and taken to a house, where she was forced to perform fellatio on her attacker. It only took a few moments for her to bite down hard. "Please God! Let me go!" he screamed. "I swear I'll never do this again!" She didn't let up, instead leading him out of the house and into the street, where he finally hit her in the head, forcing her to let go. When he showed up at Detroit Receiving Hospital for treatment he was arrested by Officer Dan Janiak of the Sex Crime Unit. He confessed, which we were grateful for, since that meant we never had to try to match the bite marks!

Another time, I was the midnight field duty officer and was with Officer Michael Harris when we monitored a call about a rape in progress at Trumbull near Warren. We were right near there, so we raced over and found a woman who told us a young black man had attacked her. She said he was wearing jeans, a brown shirt, her black shoes, and her son's green underwear on his head. I looked to where she was pointing and saw the man running toward Trumbull, so I took off after him. I'm a fast runner and I caught up to him in a parking lot, where I chased him in circles around a van. After a few circuits, I stopped in my tracks and he very nearly smacked right into me, pulling up short and falling to his knees to crawl under the van. I grabbed his feet, pulled him out, and found that he had the victim's purse, complete with her wallet, driver's license, and credit cards. Not to mention that he was wearing the exact outfit the woman had described to me, including the woman's son's underwear. He was busted.

When we went to court, I told Judge Craig Strong what had happened. Not surprisingly, the accused had a slightly different story. He said we were both walking down the street in opposite directions when we each spotted the purse under the van. We both dove to get it but he beat me to it. He claimed that I had arrested him because he was quicker than I was. Needless to say, the judge didn't buy the story.

∼

I had one of the higher profiles in the department. I was on the news whenever there was a rape or other sex crime, I gave rape prevention and awareness talks, and Executive Deputy Chief Bannon had me substitute for him at a number of public presentations. He and I got along well, especially since he was the chairman of the Domestic Violence Board for the State of Michigan, which was of mutual interest to both of us. I traveled as far as Alabama and Indiana giving presentations for him.

My supervisor, a subordinate of Bannon's, was having a problem with my high profile. Little did I realize the extent of it. One day I got a call to go down to his office. When I did, I greeted his assistant, a sergeant who was a very good friend as well as an efficient and hard worker. He had built-in radar—he knew everything and everyone, and he knew how the department really operated.

"Sit down," the supervisor said when I walked into his office. I looked at him expectantly. He folded his hands and looked at me. "What the hell do you think you're doing?" he spat. "Who the hell do you think you are?"

"Excuse me, sir?" I said, completely caught off guard.

"I'm tired of seeing your face all over the TV and hearing you on the radio. That's enough of this crap."

I was aghast. "But sir, I'm just doing my job. Am I doing something wrong?"

He proceeded to ream me out. I was flabbergasted. He wasn't complaining about the job I was doing. What he didn't like was my having a high public profile, my not consulting him when I rearranged the Sex Crimes Unit, my becoming an active part of the Oakland County child investigation, and to top it off, I was out giving public speeches on domestic abuse and personal safety. How dare I!

"If you don't stop this shit I'm going to ruin your career," he told me bluntly.

He chose the battlefield, and it was right there and right then. I'd never sworn at a superior officer, and I realized that what was about to happen could jeopardize my career, but I also knew there was no way I could back down since he was the one who fired the first shot.

"You'll what?" I asked.

"I'll ruin your career."

"Stand up," I said, suddenly becoming that kid who grew up on the lower east side of Detroit again. "Stand up and I'll kick your ass. Come on. Stand up!"

His assistant could hear this through the open door. He came over and closed it, then called Chief Hart.

"You don't talk that way to me," he barked.

"The hell I don't. You're talking to *me* that way. You told me what you're going to do to me, now I'm telling you what I'm going to do to you."

Suddenly, the door opened and Bill Hart, the chief of police, walked in. The supervisor didn't know that Bill and I had worked undercover together years before. He didn't know that Bill Hart had recently been at my wedding.

Bill's a very astute guy. He knew something was going on because I was obviously upset. "Ike, how are you doing?" he asked.

Before I could answer the supervisor looked him right in the eyes and said, "You know something, chief? I was just telling Ike, the old professor, what a great job he's doing."

I looked at him in amazement as if to say, "You pathetic soul. You're trying to worm your way out of this just to keep the chief from knowing you were doing something wrong."

Bill told him that we were old friends and diffused the situation. As I walked out of that room, Chief Hart followed me and whispered, "Give me a call at home later."

When I did, I found out what had kicked this whole thing off. It seemed that the day before the chief had been at the mayor's office with Fred Williams, who worked in Public Information, and Dan McKane from the chief's staff. As they left, they got on the elevator and ran into my wife, who worked in the budget department at the time. Fred and Bill both knew my wife because they were at my wedding. She probably gave each of them a hug. When Bill introduced her to the deputy chief as my wife, his face went ashen. Here was this very pretty white woman and she was married to a black lieutenant.

"I think that's where your problem stems from," he told me. We laughed about it, then he continued. "I'll tell you what I'm going to do, Ike. I'm going to promote you."

"Chief, you don't have to promote me."

"You've been doing a good job. I've been thinking about this for a long time. I'm going to promote you."

Well, I didn't argue long with him about this, that's for sure, especially since the next move was to inspector, which meant a sizable raise, a car, and my own command.

"Where do you want to be transferred?" he asked. This is the way Chief Hart operated—asking me where I wanted to be transferred!

"Chief," I said. "You're the one running the department and you're doing the promoting. Wherever you want to send me, I'll go."

He suggested the Special Crimes Section, which included the youth section, the child abuse detail, the major crimes mobile unit, and the gang squad.

"Sir, that would be great."

"Then figure yourself promoted."

The very next day, as I walked through the garage at headquarters where the executives park, who do I run into but my current supervisor.

"Ike, listen, about all that stuff that happened yesterday," he said, feigning remorse. "Don't worry about it. I want you to know that I've been doing some thinking and I'm recommending you for promotion."

I looked at him and thought that he must have figured I was the dumbest guy on the face of the Earth to think that he had anything to do with my promotion and not to realize that all he wanted to do was get on my good side because he knew the chief liked me. But I played along with his game.

"Why thank you, sir," I said politely, hoping he wasn't catching the sarcasm.

"In fact," he continued. "I think I might recommend that you go to the Special Crimes Section."

"Sir, I thank you even more."

"Good luck now," he said as he walked away. My mouth must have been on the ground. I was so amazed that anyone would actually stoop that low.

Thus my time in the Sex Crimes Unit was coming to an end. While I'm proud of the work I did there, and the strides that we made, there's no question it's one of the uglier jobs in police work. Now life would be easy—all I'd have to contend with was gang wars.

CHAPTER *ten*

In December of 1977, we, like most families, were getting ready for Christmas, which for us was a time of songs, laughter, feasting, and prayer. On the 15th, my mother, who was sixty-five years old, told me that the doctor wanted her to check into the hospital so he could keep an eye on her irregular heartbeat. It was nothing serious, she assured me. Just a routine procedure.

As I drove her to the hospital, I thought back to the previous August when my wife and I had broken the news that we were expecting our first child. I don't know why, but, at the time, a dark thought flashed through my mind: My grandmother Ellen had died shortly before I was born. Would our unborn son know his grandmother?

The next day, I was shocked to get a call from the hospital telling me to get there as soon as possible. I'd faced many crises during my military and law enforcement careers, but nothing prepared me for what the doctor would tell me: My mother had suffered two heart attacks and a stroke.

I thought it was a bad dream. After all, hadn't she just been in for tests? They said she wasn't responding to treatment and suggested that my sister Gloria and I speak to her, that perhaps the sound of her children's voices would bring her out of it.

We walked into the critical care unit and saw my mother lying there, tubes streaming from her nose and mouth, machines softly beeping, monitoring her feeble vital signs. "I can't see her this way," Gloria said as she turned away. I approached the bed and took my mother's hand, repeating her name over and over. There was no response. I tried again and again, but she was silent, unmoving. The doctor took me aside and told me that at her age, and in her condition, there was a strong possibility she might not recover.

"What can I do?" I asked.

"Pray for a Christmas miracle," he replied.

I walked down the hall and stumbled into the chapel, sliding into a pew. I prayed.

For the next few days, I sat at her bedside holding her hand and talking to her. I told her how Pat's pregnancy was coming along. I told her about my day in the Sex Crimes Unit. After an hour or so, I would go to the chapel and join my family: my sisters Gloria, Ada, Helen, Bernice, and, of course, my father. His prayers were always out loud. He was a deacon at the Weeping Willow Baptist Church and a deeply religious man. He would pray for my mother's recovery, ending each prayer by saying, "I pray for Jesus' sake."

Two days before Christmas, I got a call from Gloria. She was exuberant. "Guess what? Ma is up and talking," she said, almost hyperventilating.

I got to the hospital as fast as I could, finding my mother propped up in bed and talking a blue streak, having herself a good old time. She talked to us about losing weight, and about how she couldn't wait to get home so she could cook because the hospital food was so bad. She talked and she talked, happy to see everyone. She knew she wouldn't be home for Christmas, so she gave my sisters very explicit instructions about how to fix Christmas dinner exactly the way my father liked it. When I saw her doctor he smiled at me and said, "Maybe this is your miracle."

It was an incredible day. None of us had expected we would ever speak to our mother again, and there she was her usual self again. We all went home feeling very blessed.

Early the next morning—Christmas Eve—I got another phone call from the hospital. Get back here. Now.

When I arrived, I could tell from the look on the doctor's face that something was wrong. "You've got bad news," I said matter-of-factly.

"Yes," he replied. "Your mother just passed away."

As the family arrived and the tears flowed, I remembered how I'd prayed for a Christmas miracle that would save my mother—a miracle we didn't receive. Or did we? In the midst of the sadness, it occurred to me that although our mother was gone, she'd been back for a day, giving us a second chance to share our love with her.

We had our Christmas miracle after all.

CHAPTER *eleven*

In 1978, gangs and gang-related violence were on the rise. They had been problems for years, but were now becoming more prevalent, more out in the open, and more violent. As parents saw their kids become involved in gangs, they would try to solve the problem by moving to other, supposedly safer, parts of town. Unfortunately, this made the situation worse. The kids would simply start new chapters, so what was once a lower east side problem was now a citywide problem.

They had unusual names, like the Errol Flynns and the Coney Onies, the latter being derived form Corleone, from the "Godfather" movies. Most of the violence was directed at each other, though since senior citizens were easy prey, they were often targets too. Mayor Young declared that the police department was the biggest, baddest gang in Detroit and he wanted us to retake the streets. So we did.

The men and women of the gang squad weren't brutal—they were efficient. They knew the street, understood the language, and knew how to deal with young gangsters who would punk you out in a second if you were a weak cop, so you didn't dare back down. We had great officers like Dave Simmons, Rube Williams, Fred David, Franscott Fowler, and others who talked the talk and did what had to be done, short of kicking kids' butts, to make sure they wouldn't completely take over the city.

There were several really horrible incidents that had pushed the gang problem to the forefront, as well as helping seal downtown Detroit's reputation as an unsafe place for years to come. The first incident occurred on a hot Sunday night in August of 1976, when gang violence erupted on the streets after a concert at Cobo Hall by the Average White Band and Kool and the Gang. The worst incident occurred in a parking lot about two blocks from the concert when three white suburban couples were surrounded by a black gang who beat up the boys and raped the girls, right there in the parking lot in full view of thousands of people. It was a horrible crime and one of the worst days in the history of the city. It was a huge story and led to a general fear of downtown. Although some of the gang members were arrested, prosecuted, and off the streets, the fear was spreading.

It didn't help our cause when a local television station aired an exclusive interview with one of the gang leaders, "Frank Nitty" Cunningham, of the east side gang, the Errol Flynns, who had named himself after the Al Capone era gangster. While the reporter thought he was just getting a story, what he actually did was give this thug notoriety, showing him proudly talking about his exploits of being a gang leader and bragging that he could do anything he wanted to do. This did nothing but glorify the gang lifestyle to other young people.

One of the more unusual, well-organized, and profitable gangs was Young Boys, Incorporated. This well-trained group of mostly underage boys lived in various parts of the city, including the Brewster Projects and part of the 10th Precinct. The children were recruited and coerced into selling drugs for adult dealers, who knew that if they themselves were arrested they'd be put away for a long time, but if the kids were picked up they'd be back on the street within hours.

Some officers from the 10th Precinct alerted us to this gang, which had made its way to Detroit by way of New York City. You could go to any of a number of locations and find large groups of boys, ages eleven to fifteen, hawking their wares on the street corner. They were well trained, burying most of their drugs so if they were caught they wouldn't have much on them. There was an outer perimeter of kids on bikes who acted as lookouts, as well as lieutenants who oversaw the street operations. They even had gang members who provided security, as we discovered when we lost officer Bill Green. These young people were organized, armed, and dangerous. We made them a priority—not so much because we knew the extent of what they were doing, but because we saw the potential for what it could become.

We discovered that the leaders used fear and intimidation—even murder—to recruit gang members. When they moved into a new neighborhood they'd pick out the kids they wanted, usually eleven-or twelve-year-olds, and told them they were going to join. Not ask them—tell them. If they were meeting resistance they'd pick a kid and hurt him—or even kill him—as an example. Once word got around, the other kids joined quickly. Intimidation was a strong motivator. Block by block, they had spread through the 10th Precinct, then into other parts of the city.

One time we picked up a boy who had $25,000 in cash on him. There was only one place a kid could have gotten that kind of money.

"Where did it come from?" I asked him.

"Wise investing," he answered.

Dave Simmons, my sergeant at the time, and I tried to talk sense to him. "I want to see your stockbroker," I told him. "What are you, fifteen?"

"Yup."

"Do you know that if you keep selling drugs you won't live to be sixteen?"

He looked at me, barely blinking. "If I get killed tomorrow at least I know I had fifteen good years."

That has stuck with me all these years. This was the mentality we were dealing with on the street. How could we fight this attitude?

One of the more successful things we did was to go to the Housing Department and get them to let us use a vacant apartment in the Brewster area. It overlooked a courtyard area that was an open-air drug market. The kids would dig holes and hide their drugs, then hang out in the courtyard making their sales, returning to their stash to replenish their supply on hand as they needed more. It was so blatant and out of control that the people who lived there, especially the senior citizens, were terrified.

Under the cover of the late night, gang squad officers went into the vacant apartment, one or two at a time, until there were about twenty in number. By 11:00 the next morning, the drug market was open for business and in full swing. There were officers in trucks pretending to be gasmen. Others were planted as electrical workers. At a predetermined signal, the officers burst out of their hiding places, swooping down on the young kids, who were caught completely off guard. It went off like clockwork and we arrested them all.

We were good, but so were the gang's leaders. As fast as we could bust their members, they were recruiting new ones. The drug trade was flourishing and we were doing everything we could to fight it—though not everyone in the department was happy with our efforts. One day I got a call to go downtown, where a high-ranking member of the department told me in no uncertain terms that we were not the narcotics section, that we were the gang squad, and our mission was to fight gangs, not drugs. He told us to pull back.

"But sir, we're doing a good job," I explained. "There are things gang squad officers know that nobody else does, and we have them on the run."

"Your job isn't fighting narcotics," he repeated. "It's fighting gangs. You will cease and desist from those activities."

"What am I supposed to tell the officers? They're doing a great job and I have no doubt that if we don't continue this fight things will get out of control."

"It's not your job, it's somebody else's," he said, meaning the narcotics division. "You'll stop now."

This was scary, and puzzling. For the first time in my life I'd been ordered by a superior officer to stop doing effective police work. I went back and talked to Dave Simmons and other members of the squad. We were baffled. But we also knew there were forces that operated within the department that scared the hell out of us, so we stopped. There was no choice, really. As a result of that order, Young Boys, Incorporated flourished, spreading not only throughout Detroit, but into other communities as well. And I sincerely believe this directly led to the proliferation of drug trafficking in the city and to an easing of enforcement. Someone seemed to want Young Boys, Incorporated to grow. Well, he or she got what they wanted.

∾

I've always felt that even though police work is serious business, maintaining a good sense of humor and injecting levity into a situation can do wonders for everyone involved. One day I was sitting in my office at the Special Crimes Section, which was just off of the lobby, when this couple came in looking for their son whom the police had picked up. Not surprisingly, the man was irate and started screaming at the desk sergeant about how he wanted his child back, spewing one obscenity after the other. The sergeant was a nice guy and kept his demeanor, telling the man to leave before he caused too much trouble, but the man just continued ranting. Finally, hearing the hubbub out there, I approached him.

"Sir, you're going to have to keep the noise down," I told him, but this just caused him to turn his verbal assault on me. "Look, you're not getting anywhere acting like that," I continued. "Your child is probably upstairs in the child abuse unit, so let's go find him."

The three of us went upstairs, followed by two officers from the gang squad. Sergeant Dave Mays, who was in charge of that group, explained to the man why his son was being held. This set the man off again. He started screaming and yelling and ranting and raving until I finally couldn't take it.

"I'm not going to take this anymore. Get out of my building," I said, and then turned to walk down the stairs. As I did, this 5'2" guy jumped on my back and started hitting me on the head! I was 6'2½" and about 230 pounds, and the other officers were about the same size. As I struggled to keep my balance on the stairs, one of the other officers, seeing his inspector being attacked, pulled the man off, sending him bouncing down the steps, half running, half falling, losing his balance and hitting his head on a radiator at the bottom of the stairs. He went out like a light.

We took him to the hospital and he was okay. We charged him with assault for attacking me. When the case went to court, there we were, three cops each standing over 6-feet tall and weighing about 250 pounds next to this little guy who was all of 5'2" and maybe 120 pounds soaking wet. The guy admitted that he had jumped on my back—in a police station no less. The judge, Henry Heading, who was known for not mincing words, looked at him. "You know, you either have to be the dumbest guy in the world or the bravest."

"Your honor," I said, not missing a beat. "I think he's the dumbest."

CHAPTER *twelve*

I have to admit that I've been pretty lucky in the fact that I was given the chance to move around quite a bit within the department. I got to experience so many different aspects of police work in my years with the force, and most officers don't ever get that chance. I've always wondered why I moved so often, but I think that a lot of the moves occurred because I was requested to enact certain changes, I was well-spoken, and I was a good role model for the kids of the city. Whatever the reason, I really appreciated these opportunities.

I heard about my next transfer through the grapevine. Dave Simmons walked in one day and said there was a rumor floating around that I was going to be transferred. Well, it was news to me, and I was in charge, so I called my boss, Commander Ron Green, and asked him. He said he hadn't heard anything either. Still curious about where this was coming from, I called Executive Deputy Chief Jim Bannon.

"It's true. The mayor's going to put somebody else in charge of the gang squad and he's going to move you," he said.

"Did I do something wrong?" I asked.

"No, no, no," he replied. "This is a political move. But I can help you out if you want. Where would you like to go?"

"Wherever you want to send me," I said. As usual, I was easy. Besides, there were no bad jobs at the rank of inspector. Or so I thought.

I was transferred to the 4th Precinct, where I worked with Commander Ken Hady, whom I had known from my days on the mayor's security detail. I was going to be the commanding officer of the patrol division in a precinct known for its diverse ethnic makeup of blacks, whites, Hispanics, and middle Europeans, all hard-working, blue collar people. The Hispanic community, which already consisted of Mexican-Americans and Puerto Rican-Americans, was increasing quickly since the Cuban *Marielitos*—the prisoners who came over on boats—were settling in the area.

The 4th Precinct station house was absolutely horrible. It was dirty, old, falling apart, and it leaked. It was a terrible place to work, especially since the smell of some of the neighborhood businesses permeated the entire neighborhoods. I'd go into my office, close the door, and turn on the air conditioning to try and get rid of the smell but it wouldn't go away.

Before I got there, I knew that the 4th Precinct was known for a group of out of control officers who did pretty much whatever they wanted and essentially ran the precinct. They were called F-Troop. They were a prime example of right going wrong. Even though they were sworn to uphold the law, they'd drink on duty, not respond to calls, and even bring prostitutes into their squad cars. Internal Affairs had been looking into them for a long, long time. Sometimes it seemed F-Troop took it as a challenge to see how outrageous they could be and still get away with it.

One time, after a Fourth of July parade in southwest Detroit, Commander Hady and I were walking down the street. We passed a bar on Vernor Avenue and glanced inside to see two of our officers sitting at the bar drinking a beer, on duty and in full uniform. I'd never seen Ken that upset before or since. He walked in, confronted them, and ordered them back to the station. Of course, they lied and said they hadn't been drinking, but it was obvious they had been. They were suspended on the spot.

One of the more bizarre incidents occurred when an officer disappeared for a month—just flat out vanished. We couldn't contact him or find him anywhere. We went to his home looking for him. We went everywhere we could think of, but he was gone. It turned out that he was in Florida—he had decided he needed a break. I called the local sheriff, who went to where the officer was staying to give him a message from me: Show up for work or be fired. The officer stayed in Florida. In fact, he didn't even respond.

Police regulations said that if you didn't show up for work within five days after due notice you could be terminated. I tried to fire the AWOL officer but the Labor Relations Department said no, we couldn't do that because we hadn't notified him properly. This was absolute garbage. He finally came back, and shortly afterward, he shot a neighborhood kid in the back. It led to a major lawsuit against the city. The precinct was a mess.

The guys in F-Troop were as clever as they were devious. They couldn't intimidate me and they knew it, but they worked hard to get to other supervisors. They'd call them at home in the middle of the night and hang up. They'd order things through the mail and have them sent to their homes. They'd subscribe to magazines using the supervisor's name. They even sent a funeral wagon to the home of one supervisor, claiming there was a body to be picked up. One day, several of the F-Troop brought in an intoxicated man, took him to the garage, and placed him under the wheels of a lieutenant's car. Had the man not been discovered first, the lieutenant would have run him over. That's how cruel some of these guys were.

Another time, on a cold winter afternoon, an officer who was known to have a drinking problem staged a dramatic setup. He took a chair and put it in the vacant lot next to the station house, sat in it, and covered himself with snow. Then someone called the news media and claimed that a lieutenant made the officer sit out in the cold. They ran a picture of it hoping to evoke some sympathy, but it didn't work.

The men of F-Troop were very innovative, but childish, in how they tried to control the precinct. Luckily, we started to weed them out, either by terminating them or forcing them to resign. Bit by bit, F-Troop was leaving the department.

≈

There were, however, many officers in the 4th Precinct who will always remain close to my heart. Jim Stephens and Mike Harris both worked particularly hard. Then there was Randy Varney, who was killed in a traffic accident while off duty. His wife Sandy requested that her husband be buried in his uniform, but the request was denied so Lieutenant Ken Frayer and a group of officers from the precinct bought a new uniform for his burial. We also formed an honor guard at the funeral.

On another occasion Sergeant Madelyn Williams, who is black, and her partner, a white male, were investigating a crime at a local motorcycle bar. As they pulled up they saw a sign by the door that read, "No Colors Allowed" (meaning motorcycle gang colors). Her partner told Madelyn to stay in the car while he handled the investigation. As she sat in the car she began to stew, growing hotter and hotter by the minute. Boiling, Madelyn bolted from the car and flung open the door to the bar. There was no way this was going to happen in Detroit! She entered only to find her partner and everyone in the bar laughing—they knew she'd been sitting in the car thinking the sign read, "No Coloreds Allowed."

≈

When Ken Hady retired, I was put in charge of the precinct while they decided whether to promote me or wait for the next commander to be assigned there. The precinct commander has a lot of power—not only within the precinct, but on the street. He or she controls the fate of many businesses, since both business and liquor licenses were processed through the precinct commander, who had the authority to hold them or approve them as desired.

There was a bar in the precinct that was a total den of iniquity. It had dirt floors, was filthy, and had always been rumored to have a particularly bad clientele. One day I received a request from the owner to approve his liquor license. I wasn't too keen on the idea and was inclined to sit on it until I was satisfied that a thorough investigation had been completed. He called me every day like clockwork. I'd tell him we were doing our investigation, which we were, and that I'd let him know. Then he took to visiting the station. After all, he had a lot at stake—he could have been making a lot of money if he had had a liquor license.

One day he was at the station ranting and raving, raising hell because the investigation hadn't been completed and I was holding up his license.

"I don't think I'm going to approve it," I told him. "I'm not satisfied with what I've seen there."

"You know, the people that have been here in the past, well, I've taken care of them," he said. "If there's anything I can do for you just let me know. There's no reason for you to turn this down. I can take care of you."

"You don't need to take care of me, I'm good at taking care of myself," I told him, acting as if I didn't know what he was getting at. "The truth is, I'm just not satisfied and I'm not going to approve the license."

He blew up and started screaming, "I'll get my license! I'll go over your head and get my license! I swear I'll get it approved."

"No you won't," I called out as he stormed out of the building. After all, I was the one in charge of the precinct and I had final say. Or so I thought. Within a week he had his license. I don't know how he got it or what he did to get it, but it was approved somewhere else in the department.

This was another one of those eye-opening events for me—not only because it meant I had to watch out for the men beneath me, but also those above me. It was impossible to know, for certain, whom I could trust.

This wasn't the first time I'd run into this. Years earlier, when I was still in Internal Affairs, a man from Las Vegas named Larry came to Detroit to set up a gambling operation. He tried to bribe one of our officers. We called in the FBI, put a wire on the officer, and sat in a van listening when he went to meet the guy at a restaurant on Eight Mile. Larry started telling Dan, our officer, how much money he was going to give him to turn over information about police raids before they happened. He offered $75 per raid, figuring that Dan was a hungry cop. My partner, Jim Humphrey, and I sat there and heard every word. Suddenly, Las Vegas Larry mentioned a Detroit police inspector, a man whom I had worked for.

"I've known this guy a long time," he told Dan. "He once told me that the way it works is the coppers on the street get, say, fifty bucks and the guys above them get a little more. Sergeants get $75 while lieutenants pick up $150. So you should be pretty happy with what I'm offering you."

We were amazed that this small time hoodlum was naming names to an officer. But what amazed me even more was that the big investigation I had expected to take place never happened. As far as I know, it never went any farther, and since I was a witness, I would have expected to know about it if it had. That inspector retired not long afterward without any indication that he'd done anything wrong, though that's the way it was often handled in those days.

~

There was no question that my job was becoming more political. One day my clerk came in and told me a Miss Smith was on the phone.

"Tell her I'll be with her in a few minutes. I'm on the other line right now."

Jim, my clerk, was a hard-working officer who had been with the precinct a long time and certainly understood how the system worked. He looked at me as if to say, "You better be careful."

He returned a few minutes later. "She didn't like that," he said. "She's very upset and she hung up."

A short time later someone from the chief's office called. "We got a call from Miss Smith saying you wouldn't talk to her." I was amazed, first, that the chief's office would call me about something like this, but even more so, that whomever this Miss Smith was, she would lie about what had happened. I discovered that she was a mayoral appointee, one who had long used her association with Mayor Young to get whatever she wanted. She and I never did get along because I refused to kowtow to politics like that. She spread the word in the community that she was going to get me fired, but nothing ever happened.

I was getting a very bad taste in my mouth. I was thinking more and more that there were other things I wanted to do with my life, and being a political prisoner wasn't one of them.

CHAPTER *thirteen*

When I finished high school in 1961, I went straight into the military, never thinking that I'd continue on in my education. I planned on joining the police department and figured that it would be my career. After all, college was for the culturally elite. The 1967 riots changed all that, especially when the Kerner Commission report pointed out how necessary it was for those in law enforcement to become better educated in order to understand the problems and concerns of the community and learn how to do a better job. I started by taking one class at Henry Ford Community College. Then I took two. Eventually, I transferred to Mercy College of Detroit, which for me was one of the best schools around, not only because of its small class size but also for its religious background. I graduated with a double major in history and law enforcement.

That probably would have been the end of it had it not been for Jay Trefalet, an adjunct professor at the school. One night, she and her husband John, my wife Pat, and I were out together when Jay said that I should get my master's degree. I scoffed. After all, I wasn't sure how I'd managed to get my undergraduate degree, much less think about getting a master's! She insisted, and she was very persuasive. I enrolled in the master's program at the University of Detroit, majoring in criminal justice. As if working on my master's wasn't enough, Chief Hart selected me to attend a special school at the FBI Academy in Quantico, Virginia. For three months, I spent my weekdays in Virginia, flying back to Detroit on the weekend to attend classes at the University of Detroit. Somehow I survived. In less than two years, I had my master's degree in criminal justice.

It's hard to convey just how good it felt and what it did for my self-esteem. I loved school and had a real taste for higher education. No sooner had I received my master's than Jay and my wife both started asking me, "Why stop here?" Yes, they were talking about my going for a Ph.D. I thought they were out of their minds! I'm not Ph.D. material. I didn't see how I'd have the time for the intense study involved. I didn't think I had what it took to complete the dissertation. Besides, what would be my major?

My wife is a great one for preaching the need to better oneself. And trust me, she's a very persuasive person as well. So I went to visit the University of Windsor, which is right across the river, and checked out their psychology program, but to go there I would have had to have left the department and worked in Canada for about two years. I looked at other schools nearby but they didn't work for me either. Then I paid a visit to Michigan State University. I'd loved MSU for years. I had watched and listened to their basketball games in the late 1950s and early 1960s when Johnny Green played for them, and I followed their football team in the days of Bubba Smith and Carl Webster.

I met with a wonderful gentleman by the name of Dr. Eldon Nonnamaker, who later became a vice-president of the school. He gave me a tour of the campus and that was all it took—I entered their Ph.D. program. Who would have thought that a guy from the east side of Detroit whose parents hadn't even finished grade school would be pursuing a doctorate at MSU? As a student, my guidance counselor at Cass Tech once told me, "A colored boy like you isn't going to get hired by any firms. Why don't you go to the factories like the rest of your people?" Amazing things happen in this world.

I loved it. And my grades reflected it. The academic interaction stimulated me even more than I ever could have imagined. But lord, my days were long and hard. Each morning I'd wake up at 4:30 am, do some stretching exercises, and then run from 5:00 to 6:00. At breakfast, I'd spend some time with Pat and our son Jeff. At 7:30, I was off to work. At 4:15 pm, I left the police station and headed for East Lansing, arriving just in time for my 6:30 class. It was over at 10:00, I was back in Detroit by midnight, and I'd have just enough time to grab a few hours of sleep. Luckily, I don't need a lot. This was my schedule three days a week. The others were light days, where all I would have to do was homework. It was grueling, but I liked seeing the light at the end of the tunnel.

I was awarded my Ph.D. in 1981, the first of the McKinnon family to be so honored. I wished my mother could have been there to see me graduate. Unfortunately, my father was in the advanced stages of senility so he didn't understand what was going on. But my son Jeff was there along with my wife and other family members and it was wonderful.

Dr. Isaiah McKinnon, Doctor of Philosophy in Higher Education Administration!

∽

It was very hard watching my father's health deteriorate. After my mother's death, I spent a lot of time taking care of him. He was a tough man, but he had a very difficult time with her death. They'd been married for forty-some years when suddenly she was whisked away, leaving him alone and lonely. Sure, his children were there, but not his wife, his constant companion, and he became more and more reclusive. It was difficult not only because he'd depended on her to take care of things around the house, but also because his health started going downhill. He was losing his memory and his eyesight. He was having trouble taking care of himself. He was in his late 70s and wasn't as agile and mobile as he once was. It was very difficult for all of us.

We talked to or visited him every day and encouraged him to get involved in senior citizen social activities. I took him to various functions even though he was just as happy to stay home. As his health continued to deteriorate, he got to the point where he needed twenty-four-hour care. We put him in a nursing home, which was an incredibly difficult decision to make.

At 12:16 am on November 30, 1982, I received a call from the nursing home. A woman asked if I was the son of Cota McKinnon. When I told her that I was she simply said, "He's dead."

It was devastating. I suffered tremendous headaches and guilt over not being there when he died. We were now children without a mother or father. There would be no more going to visit them. Never again would I walk into the house, head to the refrigerator, and get something to eat, which was the long-standing family ritual. If for some reason you didn't do this, my mother would feel bad and Pop would say, "Boy, you look like you need to gain some weight." This from a man who never weighed more than 150 pounds in his whole life! Worse, there would be no more long conversations with my father.

I delivered the eulogy at my father's funeral. It was supposed to be a way to say goodbye, but you never really say goodbye. To this day, I find it extremely difficult to return to the family home. I drive by and look over, expecting my parents to be standing in the front door. There's so much said about the breakdown of families—black families in particular—and the lack of a father's presence. My father was always there. He worked tirelessly, had but a second grade education, and had been the victim of racism and segregation—yet he always maintained a positive attitude. He taught us that you can work hard and improve things for yourself and your family. He never espoused racism, hatred, or self-pity of any kind. He was very religious, being the head deacon in his church. He was a strong man and a strong role model.

One time, shortly before he went into the nursing home, I picked him up at the hospital. He was in pain and could hardly walk. I offered to carry him into the house, which upset him. "But Pop," I said. "You carried me once." He looked at me and proudly said, "Yes I did, Sonny. But I'm still a man."

I always tell people, if you listen to me you listen to my father; if you see me, you see my father. I may be a larger man, but I'll never be a bigger one.

CHAPTER *fourteen*

While I was commanding the 4th Precinct, I was approached about taking over the Tactical Services Section, commonly called the SWAT team. This is the elite unit that handles major events and incidents throughout the city, including, riots, bombs, and crowd control. Although I'd put myself on the personal fast track to get out of the department, this was a chance to not only learn another facet of law enforcement, but it also presented an opportunity to better myself. Of course I took it.

Our offices were near the old city airport, far away from the rest of the department. The men in the unit—and they were all men at the time—were very serious, very dedicated, and very highly trained. They were also very clever. I discovered right away that some of them had figured out that if they made an arrest shortly before their shift was over they'd go into overtime when they stayed to book the prisoner. A few of them did this just about every day, and were paid very well for booking someone they could have arrested hours earlier. I put my foot down and, as expected, they didn't like it one bit.

I always thought that, no matter what division I worked in, it was important for me to go out on patrol and be an active member of the troops. As inspector in charge of the Tactical Services Section, I'd go out with my clerk, Greg Smolinski, a 6'5" Polish-American whom I called "Smo." One summer morning at about 8:30 am, we were driving down Alter Road in an unmarked beige Plymouth. We were sitting at a light and looked over to see a black man in his mid-20s standing at a bus stop. Obviously, he hadn't noticed us because the light changed and all of the cars went through the intersection except us. He turned around and kicked in the front door of a bar. I looked at Smo. Smo looked at me. We couldn't believe our eyes. The man waltzed into the bar and burgled the place, right in front of us.

We got on the radio and told dispatch what was happening, and then went in and arrested the man for breaking and entering. He was surprised that we'd gotten there so quickly. Hell, he was shocked we were there at all! As we started to handcuff him he said, "You guys are arresting me because I'm black."

Smo looked at me. I looked at Smo. Without missing a beat, we both spoke as one: "No, we're arresting you because you're a dumb crook."

It wasn't long after joining Tactical Services when I was approached by Dr. Nicholas DeGrazia, vice president of the University of Detroit, and offered the job as director of public safety and adjunct professor of criminal justice. I'd been looking to leave the department but wasn't sure what I wanted to do. This sounded perfect. The pay was good and I'd receive my police pension on top of it, but just to play it safe, I decided that, instead of resigning, I'd take a leave of absence from the department. I went to Chief Hart, told him my plans, and he said fine. He was a great guy and we had a straight-up relationship. We agreed that on October 16, 1984, I'd start a one-year leave of absence from the department. It would be a smooth, simple transition to civilian life.

Or so I thought.

≈

Sunday October 15th, the day before I was to leave the department, was also the last game of the 1984 World Series. The Detroit Tigers were playing in it after having had a magical season, ending up with a 104 and 58 record. I remember that on the first day of the 1984 season Eric Smith, a long-time local television personality with Channel 7 in Detroit, stopped me on the street and asked how I thought the Tigers were going to do that year.

"They're going to win the World Series," I boldly predicted.

"Are you serious?"

"Yes I am, Eric. Wait until October and you'll see."

Of course, I had no idea that prediction would come true, but face it, they were my hometown team—the Detroit Tigers!

The Tactical Services Section was on alert that night. After all, we were in charge of crowd control and there's nothing like a World Series to bring out the festive rowdiness in a city. There had been small problems during the playoffs, but nothing we hadn't expected and prepared for. During each home game of the series we assigned a number of officers to Tiger

Stadium to augment the uniformed officers who were working there.

It was a chilly evening. The weather forecast was for heavy rain but we were hoping that it would hold off until after the game. Our orders were to not let the scalpers and other hangers-on loiter in front of the stadium. They could stay across the street, but we wanted to keep the immediate area clear. It was a circus-like atmosphere—people filled the sidewalk, radio stations were camped out, there was even a huge inflated gorilla perched on top of a building. It was a gigantic party, one filled with people hoping the Tigers would beat San Diego to become the world champions. The atmosphere was more electric than you can imagine. I was excited to be there even though I was on duty. It was hard not to have a good time.

As soon as Kirk Gibson hit his three-run home run off Goose Gossage, people began flocking downtown to be near Tiger Stadium. The city had set up a large television screen in Hart Plaza for those who couldn't get into the stadium and the area filled up rapidly. The game ended. The Tigers won. And people started to celebrate. As fans stormed the field, our Tactical Services officers went out to keep watch. No one wanted to stop the fans from celebrating, but it quickly escalated out of control. People ripped up the fences, tore up the sod, and threw objects around the field.

We started to try to clear the field and the stadium. Suddenly a young woman ran up behind Officer Rod Schaft and kicked him hard in the back of the knee, an injury that ultimately required several operations and caused him to leave the force with a disability. Someone threw a flashlight battery and hit my commander in the head, drawing blood. The celebration was getting ugly: People were out of control. Out of maybe 55,000 people in the stands, 54,000 of them were being orderly, but the ones who rushed the field were caught up in the euphoria and were going nuts.

Eventually we cleared the field, turning our attention to the streets around the stadium which were wall-to-wall people—Michigan and Trumbull was the place to be. Cars were at a standstill. People drove down the freeway, parked their cars on the shoulder, then climbed over the embankment so they could hang out by Tiger Stadium. Radio stations were blasting. Television stations were broadcasting live. People were swarming in from miles around to be a part of the celebration.

My first hint that something was about to go really wrong came when I saw a woman walking with her very young son. He took the pop bottle he was holding and threw it straight up in the air, applauding and cheering as it hit the sidewalk and broke.

"Ma'am," I said. "Why did you let him do that?"

"He's just celebrating and having a good time," she replied.

I knew it was about to get out of control.

Our orders were to let the people have their fun, and to let them take over the streets and get it out of their system, assuming that eventually it would quiet down and they'd all go home. So we pulled back, leaving no police presence in the area. We moved one block north to Trumbull and I-75 and bivouacked there, leaving two of our cars at the corner of Michigan and Trumbull. For one thing, it was virtually impossible to move them, since the streets were jammed. For another, it was a decoy presence, making people assume that we were in the area and keeping an eye on things.

It's hard to describe how wild, crazy, and out of control some of the people were. And it was hard to fault them completely, since I too was as excited as I could be that we had won. But I can fault them for the way that some people seem to define "celebration." Everybody just wanted to join in on the chaos. The larger the crowd grew, the crazier things got.

Someone called the department and said that a group of people was attempting to turn over a bus at Michigan and Trumbull. I took three officers and jogged over and discovered a bus from Ohio trying to get through the crowd—only the crowd had stopped it. They were rocking it from side to side attempting to tip it over! Not only were the people inside petrified, but if the bus actually had tipped over, people in the crowd would have been crushed. There were people standing on top of the bus, obviously intoxicated, cheering for it to tip over.

I opened the door to find a frightened bus driver and a group of senior citizens who were scared witless. You could see the fear in the faces— "Help us!" I did my best to reassure them, then got off the bus and started pulling people away. The crowd pushed back. Then someone punched me in the back. Someone else did the same thing to Officer Danny Ford, who used to be a boxer. He leveled the guy, hitting him in the chest and sending him sliding across the road into the crowd. That was it. That was absolutely it.

People in the crowd opened the engine compartment at the rear of the bus and started yanking out the wires, completely disabling it. We somehow managed to get a tow truck through the crowd and it pulled the bus and the poor frightened occupants to safety. I doubt if any of them have ever returned to the city of Detroit again.

No sooner had we gotten back to the bivouac area than we got a call that two police cars were on fire at the corner of Michigan and Trumbull. Knowing we'd left our cars there, we ran as fast as we could. We turned the corner and—lo and behold—there were our police cars, overturned and burning.

As I stood watching, a young man stepped out of the crowd, a guy named Bubba who was about to become famous overnight. He walked up to the overturned car, put his foot on it, and held up a Tigers pennant.

Someone snapped a photograph that was seen around the world, becoming the defining image of the riots that night. Bubba hadn't burned the cars, but he sure became the evening's poster child.

We made the decision to clear the streets. Getting in a group formation, we started to sweep through the streets. The good, clear-thinking people, who were there just to celebrate, saw the potential that something bad could happen and started to leave. But that left those who were ready to stay at any cost. We brought in the mounted police because horses are great for moving crowds. We put the horses across Trumbull and got on the loudspeaker, telling people to move.

The players couldn't leave the stadium because of what was happening in the streets. It was a huge mess. We were headed west on Michigan in formation, trying to move the crowd, when someone threw a brick that hit me in the head. It bounced off my helmet and stunned me. Thank God I had the helmet on or I probably would have been killed. To this day, I have the helmet with the dent in it. Then someone threw a bottle at me and it cut my uniform. People were out of their minds, caught up in a rampaging crowd mentality, throwing bottles and bricks, setting fires, urinating in public, doing unimaginable things.

When we finally got the streets cleared around Tiger Stadium we heard a woeful cry for help over our radios—it was the officers at Hart Plaza. Because we'd focused our forces in the area around the stadium, the rest of downtown didn't have enough officers to cope with the havoc. They were on the radio screaming for help, calling out as they were being pelted with bricks and bottles.

We amassed our troops and headed toward them. What we saw amazed us—it was as if everyone who had been at Tiger Stadium had moved to Woodward and Jefferson. We got in riot formation and started clearing the area, making our way toward the trapped officers. I don't know if I've ever seen officers so happy to see me. We swept from there through Greek Town, where the crowds were big but not nearly as unruly. By 2:00 am we finally had the streets cleared.

As I left headquarters that night, the troops were lined up, not for me, but just in formation. My friend and clerk, Greg Smolinski and I walked down the line and shook hands with each member of the Tactical Services Section. It was officially October 16th. I'd not only worked my behind off on my last day with the department, but I had worked two hours into my first day in the private sector. You can't say I didn't give the department its money's worth.

CHAPTER *fifteen*

The next morning, while the news was filled with stories of the previ-ous night's mini-riot, I went to work at the University of Detroit as director of public safety and adjunct professor of criminal justice. It was a relief being at the university. Not only did it mean not having to deal with the resulting hand-wringing and soul searching the department would be going through, but it meant I was embarking on a whole new experience, one that would take me into a completely different world. This wasn't a world of hustlers and crime and victims; it was a world of young people concerned about their education, working toward positive goals in life. It couldn't have been more different. Or better for me.

That's not to say it was a walk in the park. The university was going through its own difficult times, especially in overcoming the public per-ception that the city of Detroit was a crime-ridden, dangerous place to be. That's not exactly the image desired by a place where parents are going to send their children. There was a marked lack of respect for the public safety officers and I felt they needed additional training to bring them up to the level of competence I wanted. I had to make changes, but unlike at the police department, these would be much easier to implement.

First I had to find out just how bad the situation actually was. A couple of weeks after starting there, on a cold, rainy Saturday night in November, Detroit Police Officer Ron Sexton and I went back to the campus at night to check things out. I'd heard that public safety officers were scarce on campus after midnight and wanted to see it for myself. From 10:00 pm until 4:00 am, we roamed the campus and never saw a single officer. Not one. We set off alarms but no one showed up. We listened to the police radio that I had brought and never even heard a call for an officer. It was horrible! As the night went on, I got angrier and angrier—no one was on patrol on the entire campus.

At 4:00 am, we marched into the dispatch office to find the dispatcher sitting with his shoes off and his feet on the desk. I'll give him this much: At least he was awake. In addition to him, there were supposed to be three officers and two contractual outside security people on duty.

"Where are they?" I asked.

"Let me get on the radio and find out their location," he replied.

"Don't," I said. "Just tell them to respond immediately."

The sergeant answered immediately over the radio, almost yawning, and asked what was up. I scowled at the dispatcher.

"Sir, respond to the public safety office immediately," he said obediently.

Within two minutes the three uniformed officers showed up—walking out of the back room! Obviously, they had come through the barricaded door that led to the student union and, obviously, they had been "resting," as they had called it. It was a wet, cold night outside and not only did they not have their jackets on, but they were bone dry. They wouldn't have gone outside if their lives depended on it. Hell, I was soaked.

"Where have you been, sergeant?" I asked.

"It's nasty out there tonight, sir. I told the men they didn't have to patrol."

"Did you hear any alarms?"

"Yes, sir," he said. "But we get a lot of false alarms."

"Ten of them a night?"

"Well, a lot of times the wind sets them off."

The more he danced around, the angrier I got.

"Sir, I'll accept full responsibility for this," he said, thinking that was the right thing to say.

"You're damned straight you will. Now, where are the contractual security people?"

"Sir, they're at one of the dormitories. They're on fire watch because the fire alarm system is down."

"When was the last time you checked on them?"

"I checked on them about…"

"Now, be mindful of the fact that I've been on this campus since ten o'clock and I haven't seen any of them." He could feel his ship sinking.

We marched over to the dorm and found the men, both asleep on the floor. They were there because the alarm system wasn't working properly, so if there had been a fire they could have reported it and cleared the building. We could have had a major catastrophe.

I woke them up from their deep sleep to fire them.

"You can't fire us," they said. "We work for the security company."

"If you're not off this campus in five minutes I'll lock you up for loitering."

Then I fired the sergeant. The other officers were disciplined, which set an example for how the office was going to be run from now on. We hired some great people, did a lot of work, and helped establish the new reputation of the University of Detroit's public safety department.

~

One morning two officers came in to see me in order to file a complaint. When I asked them who they were filing the complaint against, they told me that two men had called them names the previous night.

"We were on patrol late last night when we spotted a van parked behind the engineering building," the sergeant told me. "The lights were out and the window of the building was open, so we pulled up behind the van and saw that it was empty. We looked in the open window and there were two men inside so we told them to get out. When we asked them what they were doing in there, they told us that they were alumni and wanted to come back and visit the engineering building. We told them the building was open from 7:30 am to 10:00 pm, and that if they wanted to visit they could do it then. The guys thanked us, but as they pulled away in their van we heard them call us 'stupid assholes.'"

I looked at them incredulously. These guys weren't in my office to explain why they let two obvious criminals get away, they were there complaining that they'd been accurately called stupid assholes!

~

Working at the university was a challenging, mind-expanding experience. When you're involved in the world of academia and are surrounded by people who are truly concerned about trying to solve many of the world's problems, you can't help but be inspired and feel good about the job you're doing. But it had its share of heartbreaks too.

Mandy Chandler was a great young basketball player. She and her sister Kim played on the school team together for a year before Kim graduated. Kim was on her way back to Michigan from a trip to Tennessee when she was killed in an automobile accident. I was with the women's basketball coach when the call came in from Mandy's parents saying they were on their way to tell their daughter the news. I was standing on the deck outside my office when I saw them break it to her, and watched her fall to her knees. For a long time, this wonderful, compassionate young lady would come to my office to talk, to grieve. I knew what it was like to lose a loved one and I guess she felt this understanding. As painful as it was for me to see her in this state, I was always happy that I could be there for her.

I also had the pleasure of meeting Ricky Birdsong when Nick DeGrazia, the vice-president of finance, and I went to Tucson, Arizona to interview and possibly recruit him to be the school's basketball coach. We were so impressed that there was no question we were going to hire him immediately. Ricky and I developed a long friendship that was unfortunately cut short when a racist assassin murdered him. Speaking at his funeral was another one of the more difficult things I've ever had to do in my life.

∾

In 1989, I was approached by people from the Renaissance Center in Detroit, a huge office complex that included a major hotel and retail stores, about coming to work for them. I was very happy at the University of Detroit, but I'm always intrigued by a new challenge and, I have to admit, it was financially enticing. I took the job as director of security and fire protection, working directly for the CEO, Steve Horn, who turned out to be one of the best people I've ever worked for. He was tough, but fair—a good man who worked me hard. But hard work never bothered me, and I enjoyed my time there. We upgraded the security performance and improved the perception of the Renaissance Center and of downtown Detroit.

One day a security officer rushed into my office telling me I had to turn on the news. When I did the TV reporter announced that they were about to show an incredible videotape of a police incident in Los Angeles. As I watched the tape I thought, "My God, this is reprehensible! How could that have happened?" It took me back to 1972, when I'd been a sergeant at the 10th Precinct and I saw some officers beating three kids. Only this incident happened in front of God and everyone, taped for posterity. The lights were shining on a black man who was being held by a chain around his neck while the officers beat him with their nightsticks. The man was Rodney King.

When a representative from the Los Angeles police department came on and said, "You really can't believe everything you see with these tapes," I said aloud, "The cover-up has begun." I didn't want to believe what I saw, or believe that those kinds of incidents happened. We would like to think we're beyond having police officers take those kinds of actions. As professional law enforcement officers, we're supposed to be above that kind of behavior and we're not supposed to lose control or get extreme like they did, regardless of the situation.

This resonated through the black community because, very unfortunately, a great many African-Americans could relate to it. It had happened to them, or to a friend, or maybe to a relative. In the past, many of these stories had been chalked up to rumor or exaggeration, but this tape represented hard visual evidence. And everyone in the country saw it.

The Los Angeles police department denied what we had seen. They said the officers were acting as vigilantes, not police officers. They blamed it on poor training and King's "animal-like noises." They did it, they were caught, and they should have taken their punishment. Rodney King may not have been the most upstanding citizen around, but that's irrelevant—they cheapened his life and showed how little value those officers placed on a human being.

I've always wondered how prevalent these incidents really were. I witnessed it once in 1972, but I'm sure it happened on other occasions that I didn't know about. I, like most officers, joined the department to be a public servant, to serve the community, to uphold the law, to do whatever it takes to make the community a safer place. Unfortunately, there are some who become police officers for all the wrong reasons: power, prestige, and money. And not the money you make as a salary, but the money you make on the side.

The Rodney King incident affected this country and law enforcement more than anyone could ever have imagined. Most African-Americans who are aware of American history can recall the '50s and '60s, when innocent people in Alabama and other southern states were hosed down with high-powered fire hoses and had dogs set on them. We saw films and photographs of it, but we didn't see what happened when they got to the police station and the cameras weren't around. Here it was, though, happening right in front of our eyes in 1991, in a cosmopolitan city that supposedly had one of the best-trained police departments in the country. Making matters worse, a supervisor had played an active part in it.

For a long time after that, whenever police officers would stop someone they'd hear, "You're not gonna treat me like Rodney King, are you?" Whites and blacks alike. It was a tremendous setback to law enforcement that will take years to recover from.

~

AS A LAW ENFORCEMENT OFFICER,

my fundamental duty is to serve the community; to safeguard lives and property; to protect the innocent against deception, the weak against oppression or intimidation and the peaceful against violence, or disorder; and to respect the constitutional rights of all to liberty, equality, and justice.

I will keep my private life unsullied as an example to all and will behave in a manner that does not bring discredit to me or my agency. I will maintain courageous calm in the face of danger, scorn, or ridicule; develop self-restraint; and be constantly mindful of the welfare of others. Honest in thought and deed in both my personal and official life, I will be exemplary in obeying the law and the regulations of my department. Whatever I see or hear of a confidential nature or that is confided to me in my official capacity will be kept ever secret unless revelation is necessary in the performance of my duty.

I will never act officiously or permit personal feelings, prejudices, political beliefs, aspirations, animosities, or friendships to influence my decisions. With no compromise for crime and with relentless prosecution of criminals, I will enforce the law courteously and appropriately without fear or favor, malice, or ill will, never employing unnecessary force or violence and never accepting gratuities.

I recognize the badge of my office as a symbol of public faith, and I accept it as a public trust to be held so long as I am true to the ethics of police service. I will never engage in acts of corruption or bribery, nor will I condone such acts by other police officers. I will cooperate with all legally authorized agencies and their representatives in the pursuit of justice.

I know that I alone am responsible for my own standard of professional performance and will take every reasonable opportunity to enhance and improve my level of knowledge and competence. I will constantly strive to achieve these objectives and ideals, dedicating myself before God to my chosen profession—law enforcement.

This is the law enforcement code of ethics. During my tenure in the Detroit police department, I read it often. When I was chief, I would have the officers working under me read it often. For every class of new officers that would come through the academy, I would get them to read and recite it in front of me—often.

It should be important to every police officer out there. I still get chills when I read it, and feel deeply about its importance. If an officer doesn't believe in what it says, then that officer cannot uphold the dignity of the office and it would be very easy for him to become corrupted. And believe me, there are plenty of temptations that police officers must resist—sex, drugs, money—people will offer things that you couldn't ever imagine.

One of my proudest moments occurred when an officer called me after he was approached by a fellow officer to perform an illegal act. He remembered listening to me at the academy, and the emphasis that I had put on the code, and it had really had meant a lot to him. He had made the choice to live by the code, while other officers disregard it.

Temptations will always be there, but it's easy to resist if you believe in the very basic guidelines of law enforcement. It angers me to hear of officers who live beyond it. It angers me deeply.

CHAPTER *sixteen*

My time at the Renaissance Center was good, though largely uneventful. But that changed one day in 1992 when I received a call from Dennis Archer. Rumors had been flying around the city that he was going to challenge Coleman Young in the upcoming mayoral election. Archer was a former state Supreme Court Justice who was working for the law firm of Dickinson, Wright, Moon, Van Dusen & Freeman. To many people, the very idea of his running was a losing proposition. After all, Coleman Young had been the mayor for twenty years and the conventional wisdom said that he could run for the rest of his life and never be defeated.

Archer's phone call came out of the blue. He asked me if I'd come and talk to him. When I arrived, he laid out his plans and ideas for me. He said Mayor Young had done a good job over the years, but it was time for a change, time for the city to grow in a different direction and prosper. He truly felt that he could help save the city of Detroit, make an impact, and lead the city into the future. Mayor Young hadn't yet announced whether he was going to run for reelection, but everyone assumed he would. Archer said that he was thinking about running no matter what.

We talked for three hours. I told him how my wife and I had discussed the possibility of moving from the city—a thought that hadn't entered our minds until recently. The city was dying and needed a transfusion. The infrastructure, the buildings, the homes, even the mental structure were all crumbling and the people accepted it as the norm. City services were antiquated at best. Detroit received very little federal or state support, in spite of Mayor Young's association with Jimmy Carter. There was virtually no new construction in the city, 13 percent of the adult population was out of work, kids were dropping out of school at an alarming rate, and the police department had been rocked by scandal. The perception, both nationally and locally, was that the city was dying, that people were leaving in droves. It wasn't far from the truth. People had actually put up signs that read: "Will the last one out of the city turn off the lights?"

It seemed obvious to me that it was time for a change, that Mayor Young wasn't as in tune with life on the street as he had been when he first took office. Now Dennis Archer was telling me about his ideas for change. I was moved by his plans, his ideas, his thoughts, and his obvious dedication. I liked what I saw. He told me that Neil Shine, the publisher of the *Detroit Free Press*, and Curtis Blessing, a neighbor, friend, and attorney, had both told him about me. He asked if I would help him. I said yes.

It's hard to describe how enthusiastic he made me feel. I left that meeting feeling optimistic. Here was someone who had the vision and the ideas, as well as the apparent wherewithal to make them reality. And he wanted me to be on the team! I told my wife who was cautiously optimistic. She asked me what exactly I was going to do for Archer and I said, "I'm not sure, but I do know that for the first time in my life I'm going to become actively involved in politics. I don't know what I can do politically, but I do know I can protect him and make sure he remains safe."

I told her that despite my full-time day job at the Renaissance Center I was committed to helping Archer get elected. She'd never seen this side of me, an active political side. And to be honest, I hadn't either. Pat has spent her entire career working in government, much of it with the city of Detroit. We love the city. We'd discussed the city's problems innumerable times and agreed that it was ripe for change. I think she was a little shocked when I told her that unless Dennis Archer got elected we'd be moving our family out of Detroit. Since there was no way I wanted to do that, I made a commitment to try to get the one person elected who I felt could make the changes the city needed: Dennis Archer.

∼

Archer started holding strategy meetings in his basement. I sat and listened, not knowing many of the people in the room. I'd seen some of them before, however, and knew they were politically active. When he got around to outlining our job positions I spoke up and told them I'd make it my job to ensure that the candidate and his family were safe. I said I'd recruit people from the department to volunteer, and make sure that he'd have around-the-clock protection. And that's what I did.

Word spread quickly that I was handling Archer's security, and the phone started ringing off the hook at the Renaissance Center. I heard from members of the department who were calling from safe phones, pay phones, anyplace where they could be assured of privacy, since they were afraid that if it were discovered they were associating with me or Dennis Archer they'd suffer backlash from the administration. The election was a long way off, so I told them that if they were serious about giving some type of commitment, they should lay back until it got closer to the election, and then come out and show their support.

During that first year I was with Dennis Archer practically every day. Wherever he went, I was there. We talked a great deal and we both learned a lot. It was a sacrifice on all of our parts, but I felt the sacrifice was necessary for the good of the city. Public response to Dennis was growing. The more he talked to people, the more they lined up behind him. It was electric. The day Archer officially announced his candidacy at the Gem Theater in downtown Detroit, George Crockett, a longtime congressman, judge, and civil rights advocate who had been an ardent Coleman Young booster, threw his support behind Dennis Archer, calling on Young to retire. I remember standing in that theater and realizing that something major was happening. And it was.

We started campaigning hard. Those who loved Coleman Young and clung to the things he'd done for the city in the past detested Dennis Archer. Others didn't like him because they felt he was a black man turning against another black man and they didn't think that was right. But there were a lot of people who knew the city needed a change, an infusion of new blood, and they realized Archer was the man who could bring it about.

It was easy to see how he instilled this confidence in people. He's an intelligent, articulate, highly educated man who is always well dressed. His approach to problems was about as opposite to Coleman Young's as you could get. He wasn't confrontational, but rather judicious, pondering questions and possible solutions before coming up with his answer. He spoke like the lawyer he was, giving proper gravity to things, much like the State Supreme Court Justice he had been. Sure, there were those who preferred the confrontational style of Coleman Young, but the more Archer ventured into the neighborhoods, the more the community started accepting him—particularly the senior citizens. I had presumed this was a group that might be heavily in favor of Young, since they had long-standing ties to him, but that wasn't the case at all.

∾

On June 22nd, Coleman Young announced that he wouldn't run for another term as mayor, throwing the field wide open. Art Blackwell, chairman of the Wayne County Board of Commissioners, and Sharon McPhail, chief of screening and district courts for the Wayne County Prosecutor's Office, each announced their candidacy. The Young camp eventually threw their support behind McPhail, apparently because Archer hadn't gone to Coleman Young to seek his approval to be anointed as his successor. Archer was independent, and stayed that way. When the primary votes were counted, Dennis Archer had the top slot, followed by Sharon McPhail. The election was on.

It quickly turned nasty. Rumors flew. Almost anything you could imagine being said was said about one candidate or the other. Everything was being analyzed in depth. During one debate, McPhail said something that angered Archer. Dennis stopped and paused for about ten seconds before answering. The press made a huge deal out of it, claiming that Archer was indecisive, when the truth was that he paused because he knew that if he spoke quickly it would have been out of anger and he wanted to calm himself and maintain his dignity, which is the way he operated. We laughed about it later, saying maybe he should have taken the Coleman Young approach and used an expletive.

Dennis Archer remained a gentleman throughout the campaign. He's a scholarly man, a family man, and a decent person. Where Young was the consummate confrontational politician, Archer was the levelheaded, reserved gentleman. I can't remember an instance where he was negative, even when someone else gave him a hit. I'll always respect him for maintaining his dignity. One time, after someone had taken a potshot at him, I asked him how he maintained his dignity through it. He said, "If, in fact, I said what I wanted to say, all the people who respect me for how I carry myself would lose that respect." He was right.

≈

I was working long hours, spending my days at the Renaissance Center and working long into the night and all weekend with Archer. Luckily, I had a great CEO at the Center who let me take the time off to be a part of the campaign. I recruited a group of volunteer security people who believed in the cause. I also had some who were doing it because they saw a potential winner and wanted to ride his coattails, hoping it would be good for their career. Many members of the police department wanted to get involved but were afraid to come out publicly and take a stand, and for good reason. Dave Simmons, who was an inspector at the time, openly supported Archer. So did my old friend Frank Mitchell. Others still needed secrecy. I held secret meetings. It was funny in a B-movie sort of way. They'd call me from a pay phone and set up a meeting place. Then, under the pretense of going to a restaurant, they'd meet me in a hotel room or banquet hall and we'd talk about the state of the city, and of the department, and what could be done to improve them if Archer won the election. One guy went so far as to change into civilian clothes, donning a hat and sunglasses to sneak into the Renaissance Center. I arranged for some of these people to meet with Dennis Archer, and helped put together what would become a strong team with common goals.

~

Election day was tough. Richard Dickerson, a life-long friend whom I'd grown up with, died two days earlier while waiting for a heart transplant, leaving a wife and young daughter. On election day morning, I spoke at his funeral service, then went downtown to pick up Archer. Together we went from polling station to polling station, school to school, traveling through the city doing some last-minute campaigning.

That night, those of us who were closely involved in the election went to a suite at the Westin Hotel in the Renaissance Center to watch the election results with Archer, his family, and friends.

Early reports showed Archer in the lead. By about 8:00, they were predicting a huge victory. We were ecstatic!

The celebration party was in the large ballroom in the hotel. I'd planned to bring the mayor-elect down in the elevator and enter through a rear door. Someone suggested we change that, as it would make more of a splash for the eleven o'clock news if he walked in the front door to a cheering crowd. I went downstairs and checked out the room. It was packed. Wall-to-wall people. I went back upstairs and advised the mayor-elect not to enter the front door because, with the crowd, it would have been next to impossible to make it through the gauntlet of hands and well-wishers. While we were discussing this, the phone rang continuously and people kept showing up at the suite. Some of them were people from the department who had been reluctant to show their support. All of a sudden they were standing at the door.

My decision stood. We would take the mayor-elect in through one of the ballroom's side doors, figuring the crowd would be surprised. We'd get the desired reaction, yet we'd be able to navigate our way to the stage reasonably well. I told Dave Simmons to stand up on stage next to the mayor-elect. Dave laughed. "Look," I told him. "This is going to change your life forever. You'll be seen by everyone, standing right next to the mayor-elect. Before you know it, people in the department are going to envision this awesome power that you have. By morning, you'll be getting hundreds of calls." And boy, was that ever prophetic!

We took the elevator down, got off at the fifth level, and walked through the corridor to the side door. The room was packed, music was playing, and the crowd was in a celebrative mood. I led Mrs. Archer and the rest of the family through the crowd. I literally lost my breath. I was completely caught up in the euphoria of the moment and the import of what I was involved in, and it was fabulous. We made our way to the stage, but the number of people who actually jumped up there to be close to the mayor-elect concerned me. It was a security nightmare. Archer gave a great speech, and my man, Dave Simmons, was right by his side. I've never seen another night like it.

~

While all this was going on at the Westin, I had something else on my mind: a room across town. An undercover officer I knew had contacted me, swearing that in past elections people from Mayor Young's special detail would sneak into the room at Cobo Hall where they stored the absentee ballots and tamper with them. I had a hard time believing this. After all, this is Detroit, not some Hollywood political thriller. To be safe, though, I sent some of my volunteers, all off-duty cops, to keep an eye on things, telling them to position themselves at every entrance. This was, of course, in addition to the uniformed men who were already there on duty.

It didn't take long before someone showed up and told my officers they weren't allowed to be there and had to leave. We never knew who sent them. My man in charge refused. A call went in to the department in an attempt to force my officers to leave, but no one would budge. All night these officers stood guard, making sure that no one entered or left the room. And all night, they watched a steady stream of cars drive by slowly, checking out the situation, then drive off. No one knew for sure what their intentions were, but it certainly appeared as if they were trying to do something sur-reptitiously. Whatever it was, we stopped them dead in their tracks.

~

Once the election celebration wound down, we went back upstairs to the mayor-elect's suite. We were basking in the glow of the night and fending off unannounced visitors. I swear you could almost see the skid marks on the shoes of those who made a mad dash trying to get to the Renaissance Center, most to see Dennis Archer, though some were from the department looking for me. It was too funny.

We were getting ready to leave at about 3:00 am. Archer told me he'd be having breakfast the next morning at the New Detroiter on Jefferson Street and would then drive to Lansing to meet the state legislators.

"Well, I hope you have a good time," I told him.

"No," he replied. *"We'll* have a good time."

I smiled. We'd started this journey together and there was no question that we'd be continuing it together. So the next morning, after about an hour and a half of sleep, we took off for Lansing. But I didn't feel the least bit tired. The euphoria wasn't even close to wearing off.

That night, after another long day with Archer, Dave Simmons called me at home. He was laughing almost hysterically. "Ike, Ike, Ike. What have you done to me?"

"What are you talking about?"

"Man, I've been getting calls all day from people in the department trying to get close to me, people who never even talked to me before. I had a deputy chief call and offer to take me to a football game. Another one wants to take me to lunch."

I laughed. "Better you than me, Dave. Better you than me."

≈

I continued handling security for Mayor-elect Archer while he assembled his administration. It was just natural that when you'd worked with someone as closely as I had, in the back of your mind you entertained thoughts of getting an appointed position, but, to be honest, that wasn't foremost in my mind or in my motives. The obvious place for me was as chief of police, but in all sincerity I didn't want the position. I knew that I wanted to effect some change within the city. There was a perception that the people were poor, the city was unsafe, and the police department was ineffective. I strongly felt that Dennis Archer could bring these changes to fruition, and working on his campaign was my way of helping out. But chief of police? I was happy as director of security for the Renaissance Center. It was interesting, challenging work, and it paid well. I really wasn't sure if I had any desire to get back into the public sector.

During the campaign, there had been a steady string of people who were after the job. Some had asked me to introduce them to Dennis, which I did. A few of them I had actively sought out, knowing that they'd be good for the job. One time, I did that, and Dennis looked at me funny: "Now why in the world did you introduce that person to me?" Maybe I was naive, but I was surprised when he hinted that I should consider the possibility of becoming chief.

Not surprisingly, rumors had circulated during the campaign that I was in line for the position. Even Pat heard them. We'd talked early on about how I wanted to see Archer elected, but didn't want to be involved afterward, except maybe in an advisory capacity. She made it plain that she wasn't keen on the idea of my getting back into the public sector. Or "us," as she would say, knowing that a decision like that wasn't personal—it would affect the whole family. Pat was very concerned about the stress—both on me and on the family—that would go along with this, knowing that I'm incapable of giving less than my all to anything I do.

In August, in the midst of the campaign, we'd taken our annual vacation trip to North Carolina's Outer Banks. One night, as sunset approached, Pat and I were sitting in our beach chairs, somehow finding some time alone, watching the shadows lengthen on the beach while the blazing sun sank behind the sound. I'd spent a lot of time during that vacation writing a departmental reorganization plan for the campaign, and Pat asked me about it. The conversation quickly turned to the possibility of my becoming chief.

"Why would you want to leave private industry?" she asked. I knew she was thrilled that I had moved from government to the quasi-governmental job at the university and then the mostly private Renaissance Center.

"You know, sometimes people have a higher calling to public service."

She looked at me, knowing there was no arguing with that, knowing that a big part of me was yearning for it. We agreed, though, that any final decision would be a family one.

~

No sooner had Archer won the election than the phone started to ring with people encouraging me to become chief. One of the first calls I received was from a very prominent attorney. "Ike, the department needs you. The city needs you. It's time we had a major change around here."

I shared this with my wife and we realized that we needed to deal with this. Pat and I had planned a short post-election trip to Acapulco so we could have some time together and to celebrate my fiftieth birthday, something we hadn't gotten to do properly because between work and the campaign I barely had time to breathe, much less have a party. We stayed at the Las Brisas resort, where we had our own little pool overlooking Acapulco Bay. It was stiflingly hot, but a wonderful place.

We talked at great length about whether I should apply for the job as chief of police. Pat told me about the night of the election when she drove to the Renaissance Center with our son Jeff so that he could be a part of the celebration and euphoria. As they pulled into the underground garage, she told Jeff that I was considering applying for the job as chief and had asked him what he thought.

"You know, Mom," he said. "I keep thinking that there are a lot of drug dealers in this city and that the police officers who go out and arrest them, well, the drug dealers don't remember who they are. But you know they're going to remember who the chief of police is, and we live in a house with floor-to-ceiling glass windows. How are we going to feel safe?"

It was interesting that while Pat's and my primary concerns had been the time commitment, the loss of family time, and the stress the job can put on our health, we hadn't given a lot of pause to the question of the family's safety. Since Jeffrey and Jason had been six years and six months old, respectively, when I retired from the department in 1984, they had little or no recollection of me as a police officer or the effect it can have on family life.

Basically, Jeff was against it, Pat was for it with stipulations, and Jason, well, he was eight going on nine years old and he had his own outlook on the situation.

"Dad?" he asked me one day. "Does the chief get any special deals on stuff?"

"Well, maybe," I told him.

The kid didn't miss a beat. "Take the job."

~

Pat and I hashed it out—while fully enjoying Acapulco, of course!—and agreed that if I was, in fact, offered the job as chief of police, I would accept it only on the condition that it didn't interfere with my health or take away from my time with the family. We knew that when you take a position like this your life changes—not only in terms of the job you're doing, but also with the public and media scrutiny that comes with it. Everyone wants to know you and wants you to come to their events, and there's only so much a person has to spread around. Before you know it, all you have is a public life and your private one ceases to exist. One of the stipulations we made was that this wouldn't happen. We had our priorities and we wanted to keep them intact.

Another important agreement I later reached with the mayor-elect was that I be given the autonomy to put my staff together and run the department as I saw fit without political pressure or influence. As a part of the plank I'd written up the previous summer—which showed that even though I hadn't applied I was still taking it seriously—I'd put together a list of the team I thought should be in place. When I talked to the mayor-elect about this he agreed that I'd be able to choose whomever I thought would do the best job.

I applied. The interviews went great. On December 6, 1993, I got the call from Dennis Archer.

~

No sooner had I agreed to accept, than his staff started calling people to set up a press conference for the next day. It was to be the first in a series in which the mayor would announce his appointments. Mine was first, since he wanted to demonstrate to the people of the city that public safety was a top priority.

Someone, whether it was deliberate or not—I'll never know—tipped off the media. Emery King of WDIV-TV Channel 4 ran it as the lead news story that evening. Pat got home from work a little after 6:00 and the phone was ringing off the hook, which was how she found out about the impending press conference. Even though she knew I was going to accept the job, she hadn't known any other details, so, in good conscience, she was able to tell the reporters that she didn't know a thing about any press conference or announcement. In the midst of all the media hounding, I called her from Dennis Archer's basement and filled her in on the details.

The reporter Pat had to deal with most was James Titsworth of the *Detroit News*. He knew that the *Detroit Free Press* had a story ready to run and, of course, he wanted one too, so he kept calling, trying to get someone to confirm the appointment. Since I spent most of the evening at Archer's, Pat was fielding all of his calls. When I got home at about 11:00 pm, I found Pat running around the house being supermom, sewing on buttons, washing and ironing a good shirt for me to wear, and shirts for the boys too. Because there was still an official lid on the story—even though it was all over the 11 o'clock news—Pat continued running interference by answering the phone.

Titsworth was persistent. Sometime around 1:00 am, when we were already in bed, he called for a final time, begging to talk to me. "My God, Ike," Pat pleaded. "Please confirm something for this reporter or he's going to call us right through until tomorrow morning and we'll never get any sleep."

I relented. "Listen, if the *Free Press* has a story about this, why don't you just go with the same news they're running?" That was all he needed to hear.

The next day, when Pat got home from work, there were a dozen red roses waiting for her from Titsworth with a note apologizing for bothering her so much the night before.

~

We awoke the morning of the press conference to find a TV crew from Channel 2 on the front lawn. The *Detroit Free Press* had done a long interview with me by Jack Kresnak, who had been perceptive enough to talk to me the week before "just in case." And there was Titsworth's article in the *News*. We were running around the house getting ready to go to the Bates Academy to be a part of something that would dramatically change our lives. We had debated whether the boys should miss school to go, and wisely decided that this was a historic day for the family and they should be a part of it.

Later, as we followed the mayor upstairs in the Bates School, we were blinded by the lights for the cameras. There were people in the passageway, the hallways, the doorways, spilling out into the corridors as we made our way to the gym.

CHAPTER *seventeen*

I quickly put my executive team together. I knew it wasn't enough for us to change the perception of the department. We had to change the reality of how it operated. Two high-ranking members of the department under the previous administration had gone to jail: Chief Hart, who had received a ten-year sentence for embezzling $2 million in police funds, and his deputy chief, Ken Weiner. Needless to say, I was extremely disappointed about Chief Hart's sentence. Although he had been convicted, it wasn't easy to see my good friend go to prison. Based on rumor and innuendo, I'm positive that there were more people involved within the department, and that Hart took the fall for all of them. Still, what he did was totally inexcusable.

We needed to move away from the political patronage system, to seek out individuals who were not only well educated and experienced, but dedicated to bettering the department and city. It was important to put together a team that made decisions based on the law and on the needs of the community, rather than on political considerations.

It was incredibly difficult having to tell people in high-ranking positions that I appreciated their years of service, but was replacing them, often with people who were under their command. Some of them had held command positions since before I joined the department. But it was necessary, especially if we were going to effect an immediate change of direction in the department. It meant surrounding myself with people who were attuned to that change, people who had the dedication, the insight, and the ability to accomplish the goals at hand. Some of the old guard were understanding. Others left without saying a word to me ever again. Still others showed an obvious disdain for me and for those who replaced them. But I did what I felt had to be done for the good of the department and the city.

I eliminated the rank of executive deputy chief. Instead, I appointed five deputy chiefs. Each of them held either a Master's Degree or a Juris Doctorate and had attended either the FBI National Academy or Northwestern School of Staff and Command. I depended heavily on this team to advise and assist me in the selection of their subordinate command personnel and in the restructuring of the department, and we did it with complete autonomy and without any outside or political influence.

～

Inauguration day was long, but fun. It started off with a breakfast at Cobo Hall, where a number of people spoke, including the Reverend Jesse Jackson. Thousands of people filled the hall while Pat and I, accompanied by our good friends Kathy and Dr. Alex Dekovich, sat in a prominent place by the podium. Afterward we went to an ecumenical mass at Blessed Sacrament Church. About midway through the service, as I was taking in the proceedings, all I could think about was how much I needed to go to the bathroom. I looked around, and then stood up, suddenly noticing that everyone was looking at me. "What are they all looking at me for?" I thought as I walked down the aisle. People were waving and smiling. When I left the bathroom, people were gathered around the door, waving, shaking my hand, and taking my picture. Suddenly it dawned on me: "Wow, I'm the chief now!"

After the service Jesse Jackson walked up to me, shook my hand, and said, "Give me a call, let's chat." Of course, I didn't have Jackson's phone number, so I was not sure how I was supposed to call, but it was a nice play on his part.

There was a brief reception at the Detroit Institute of Arts followed by the swearing-in ceremony at the Fox Theatre. Pat, Jason, Jeffrey, two friends from California, Will and Tina O'Sullivan, and I were sitting together in the second row, right behind the mayor and his family. It was exciting to hear Aretha Franklin sing the national anthem, but the most moving part was when the mayor's son, Denny, introduced his father. The mayor stood at the podium kissing and hugging his son; there wasn't a dry eye in the house. Men in general—and men of color in particular—aren't known for such open displays of emotion, and it was a refreshing change.

That night we danced at the inaugural ball in Cobo Hall until our legs were aching. The next morning, I went into my new office and got down to work. Within days, I was deep in my first crisis.

~

"Do you know who Nancy Kerrigan is?" Dave Simmons asked as he rushed into my office.

"Well, yes," I said. "She's a world famous figure skater. Why?"

"She was just attacked at Joe Louis Arena."

Immediately, I thought that she'd been sexually assaulted. "Oh my god, we're just a few days into this administration and already it's starting." Fortunately, she hadn't been sexually assaulted, but rather struck across the knee—not to insinuate that anyone getting hit on the knee is lucky. We jumped in a car and raced through the driving snow to Joe Louis Arena, only to find out that it had happened next door at Cobo Hall. Kerrigan was already gone when we got there, apparently having been taken to Hutzel Hospital, which I thought was odd, since Hutzel is a maternity hospital.

As we were starting to leave, an out-of-town newspaper reporter walked up to me. "You're the chief, aren't you?"

"Yes."

"What does this say about the city of Detroit, to have a person attacked in broad daylight at a public skating event?"

This was my first incident as chief. I knew that whatever I said next would be taken as a reflection of my capabilities as well as those of the department and the city. I paused, gathered my thoughts, then said, "We don't know yet if a crime has occurred. If and when we do find that a crime has occurred, we will investigate it to the best of our ability, leaving no stone unturned, to find the culprit. I'll get back to you with that information at the earliest possible moment."

The reporter did a double take, as if to say "Jesus, this guy knows what the hell he's doing."

I handed him my business card. "Here's my number. Give me a call later." Then we jumped in the car and took off for Hutzel Hospital.

On the way, we received a call telling us that Kerrigan was actually at the Westin Hotel, which is in the Renaissance Center, only a few blocks from Cobo Hall. We were met by Larry Alexander, CEO of the hotel, who was with Kerrigan's father.

"Where's your daughter? And how is she?"

"She's upstairs in the pool trying to work the kinks out of her leg," her father told me.

"Who's with her?" I asked.

"Nobody."

We raced up to the second floor—Dave Simmons, Greg Smolinski, a couple of security men from the Renaissance Center, and I—and checked the pool, finding it empty.

My fears were growing as I started to speculate that whoever had hit her had returned and drowned her. All this after only a few days as chief!

We had the pool manager check out the ladies' locker room. It was empty. So was the men's. There was a running track outside the pool that had a straight drop over the edge into the river and we looked there. Where was she? Was she okay?

We went back inside and her father walked in, explaining that he had found her upstairs in her suite. We ran up there and found her, sitting with her right leg extended on an exercise table with an ice pack on it. She explained to me that, as she left the skating rink after practicing her routine, a man struck her on the right knee with a pipe. Puzzled, but determined to get to the bottom of this crime, I assigned officers to guard her.

I realized that I had an international story on my hands, the likes of which the city had never seen. And once again the reputation of the city was very much at stake. I called the mayor to let him know what was going on. The department worked closely with Special Agent in Charge Hal Helterhoff of the FBI, John O'Hare of the Wayne County Prosecutor's office, and the State Police investigating the case. The next day we got a tip, which led us to Shawn Eckardt, Tonya Harding's bodyguard, his acquaintances Derrick Smith and Shane Standt, Harding's husband, Jeff Gillooly, and ultimately Harding herself.

The next morning I found myself on the "Today Show" with Katie Couric. The interview wasn't much, since there wasn't a lot I could tell her. But from a public relations standpoint it was great. It showed the people of Detroit and the world that we were on top of things, that we could work closely with other law enforcement agencies, and that we weren't the drug-infested murder capital of the world we were made out to be. It certainly helped that the perpetrators weren't local.

This set a new tone for the Detroit police department. Not only did we solve the crime quickly and efficiently, but for the first time in a long time we worked closely—and well—with other law enforcement agencies. This came in handy, since it wasn't long before the G7—the Group of Seven Industrialized Nations, met in Detroit. President Clinton, the six other world leaders, their staffs, and their security were there and we were in the spotlight again. We worked closely with the Secret Service, the FBI, the prosecutor's office, and the State Police, and it went off without a hitch.

~

As soon as my first trial by fire died down, I held a meeting of my command personnel. It was important to me that we all work together as a team, and with 4,600 people in the department, both sworn and civilian, that meant coordination. A precinct commander could have 200 officers working for him or her, and each of those officers was responsible for the 200,000 people who lived in that precinct. If we all weren't on the same page, we'd be in trouble.

I told the precinct commanders that they were expected to work a full eight-hour day. This sounds obvious, but in the past it had become common practice for some of them to come and go as they pleased, often only putting in a few hours a day. I told them they were expected to be more proactive, to seek out and meet with the business community. They were to go to the schools and talk to the principals and faculty, and listen to their ideas and concerns. They were to find out where the young people hung out, talk to them, and meet with the people of the community. These were very simple concepts to me, because once you realized that a great percentage of the crime was being committed by young people, there was no question that we needed to rally the community and solicit their help to aid in its prevention. They needed to be involved. This is the very essence of community policing.

"Thursday is no longer golf day," I told them. "And you *will* be at work. You're going to check on your people in the afternoons, in the evenings, and after midnight. You're going to make sure you have in-service training for your officers and you'll attend roll call. You'll talk to your officers and to the people in the community. Your cars aren't personal vehicles and will only be used for official business. You'll monitor your officers' sick time and their response time to calls. And you'll document every bit of this. Each of you will ride in a patrol car on a regular basis for a minimum of four hours per week so you can maintain a feel for what's happening on the street, and that includes me. Finally, don't even think about getting someone you know to go to the mayor to help you get promoted. It won't work anymore. The mayor's behind me 100 percent on this and will let me know if anybody does this. Try it and I will guarantee that you will suffer my wrath."

They looked at me in disbelief. Some figured that it was lip service and that once the meeting was over it would fall by the wayside, and in no time at all they could be back to business as usual.

I gave them fair warning that I'd be having individual meetings with them starting in thirty days, and I did. The first person I called in was surprised. "You were serious!" he said incredulously. I asked him what he'd done for roll call training. He hadn't done a thing. I asked him how many schools he had in his precinct. He didn't know. "Who are the school officers?" He had no clue. "When was the last time you attended roll call?" No answer.

I let him go on the spot.

This sent shockwaves through the department, all the way from the top to the bottom. Word was out that I wasn't kidding around, that I was serious about making changes in the department. Now they knew that I meant it. No one had done this before and it upset a lot of people. Some of them had been coasting along, making good money, driving a city car with free gas, and controlling their own clock, getting away with it as long as they contributed politically and didn't upset someone who was closer to the mayor than they were. Suddenly here I was telling them they had to be on time, be accountable, go to meetings, make sure their people were trained, keep activity log sheets, and watch their sick time. I wanted them to be a nicer, kinder, gentler command personnel and—yes, dammit—they were going to do it.

As word spread about what happened to that first commanding officer, they all started wondering who was going to be next. They unionized, which they'd discussed for years, and it was actually a good thing since it brought them closer together. This wasn't easy for me. Many of them had been friends and associates for years, but I'd watched the police department become stagnant, and when that happens the entire city suffers. I looked at running the police department as a business. We were performing a service for the people of Detroit, and if we ran our business successfully, we would turn a profit—the profit being that the people of the city would be happier, safer, more comfortable, and feel better about their city and their police department. It's ironic that Detroit is home to some of the largest corporations in the world, yet we hadn't learned from them: no one had thought to run the police department as a business.

The mayor and I had discussed, at length, the problem of people's perception of the city versus the reality. People were refusing to visit the city, saying that it was a dangerous, crime-infested place and that they felt like they were taking their life into their hands if they visited. I had personally heard people who lived in the surrounding areas brag that they hadn't been in the city limits in twenty-five or thirty years! It would be hard to shake those beliefs, and the emotions that went with them. But the time I'd spent in the community campaigning with Dennis Archer made me acutely aware that both the city and the suburbs were filled with people of all ethnicities who wanted to see Detroit succeed. Unless we could make people feel safe and realize that it wasn't as bad as they thought or had been told, the city would continue to decline.

I made it a point to educate the surrounding communities about our efforts to effect a positive change. Both blacks and whites from the suburbs were reluctant to venture into Detroit, yet they kept saying they wanted to come back. I spoke to two thousand people at a prayer breakfast at Cobo Hall, giving a plea for reconciliation between the city and the suburbs. It was well received. Afterward, I was invited by a number of surrounding communities to speak to them. I started receiving more and more calls to speak on radio, on television, and to community groups. It quickly got to the point that I would sometimes give three or four talks a day. Mayor Archer and I, along with others in the administration, became bridge builders to understanding. The message was popular, and we were determined to preach it to anyone who would listen.

CHAPTER *eighteen*

From the very first day Dennis Archer held the press conference announcing that I would be chief of police, most of the media were fair and supportive of us. I think they were ecstatic over having public officials who were open, honest, and willing to talk. The people of the city picked up on this and seemed to appreciate that I came across as a straightforward person, someone who's honest, personable, sincere, and dedicated to making a change. And I spoke for them.

I knew that the number one problem in Detroit was drugs. Youth crimes, stolen cars, carjackings, and homicides were major issues too, but it was crucial that we make an impact on the drug trade. I put Rudy Thomas, my deputy chief, in charge of this problem, coordinating the Violent Crime Task Force and the narcotics division with the FBI, the DEA, and the State Police. Thanks to everyone's hard work, we saw a tremendous increase in the amount of drug seizures and the number of arrests and convictions.

My executive team identified, and made recommendations, about dramatic cuts that could be made in the department, which was top-heavy with executives. Deputy Chief Rudy Thomas and Commander Frank Mitchell discovered buildings that the department had leased that had high-rent, long-term contracts. I cancelled a number of them. There was a long-standing policy that certain members of the department could drive unmarked police cars while off duty, which added to the wear and tear on the fleet, not to mention the price of gas. I ordered a reevaluation, permitting only authorized on-call personnel to take a vehicle home. I did this out in the open, very publicly, making sure the people of Detroit could see what I was doing. They quickly discovered I was just as ready to air our dirty laundry as the clean.

I made it a policy that in order to reach the executive ranks it would be mandatory to have an undergraduate degree. This had never been done before, and again it created bad feelings among those who disagreed with the changes. It wasn't that I held anything against anyone who hadn't finished college, but rather I felt strongly that we should be setting a good example. They all had to attend either the FBI Academy or the Northwestern School of Staff and Command to learn management skills. After all, my plan was to be chief for no longer than two or three years, and I was determined that I'd not only leave the department in better shape than I found it, but that I'd make sure those under me were prepared to step into place and present a better police force.

As a group, the executive team and I decided that I'd be the point person for the department. There would always be a Public Information Office, but we felt it was important for the public to have a visible, recognizable person, face, and voice that they could count on seeing when the media reported on what was happening in the department and around the city. If something major occurred, I'd be there, no matter what time of day or night.

To be perfectly honest, it was tiring. For the first year or so, I was running on pure adrenaline, as was Greg Smolinski, my driver and constant companion, who was with me pretty much all the time. It was considered a minor miracle if I grabbed more than five hours of sleep on any given night that year. If there was a function at noon, I'd be there. If there was somewhere I should be at midnight, I'd be there. The public seemed reassured that the chief of police was visible and approachable. I had people tell me that if something bad happened they'd turn on the television and wait for me to come on and tell them exactly what occurred, comforted by the knowledge that no matter how bad it was I would be open and honest with them. That's not to say everyone loved me, but I honestly believe most people saw my concern and interest and it rubbed off.

We set up a system where one of my deputy chiefs and I would double-team major incidents. For example, one of them would go to the scene of the crime, while I'd go to the hospital where the victim or an injured officer had been taken. It worked well because people grew to trust us.

∼

What I didn't bargain for was becoming a semi-celebrity. It's not easy going from being an anybody on the street to being one of the most recognized people in the city. A great number of people wanted to talk with me. It was overwhelming at first. People would walk up, shake my hand,

and ask for an autograph. Some even wanted me to kiss their baby! I didn't understand it: I was the chief of police, not a rock star.

There was no question that people were looking for a hero. As chief of police, I was probably the second most visible person in the city, and I was very active in the community, maintaining a high profile in the media and on the street. They loved it. I think there was trust because I wasn't a politician. I was just me, a dedicated and sincere public servant. When a young girl was killed on Christmas Eve, I organized a fund-raising drive for her family. When a child was injured or killed, I'd be there to offer support and encourage the community to help. I spent the night consoling the family of a boy who had drowned in the river. People saw this, liked it, and grew to expect it. I attended more funerals than a person should have to, and I spoke at many of them. It had never been like this before and the community embraced it and me.

I prided myself on being open, visible, and accessible—so much so that I would answer my own telephone. One day I picked up the office phone and heard a woman's voice say she wanted to talk with "that goddamned chief."

"I can help you, ma'am." I told her.

"Look, damn it, I want to talk to that goddamned Chief McKinnon."

"Ma'am, I think I can help you."

"I don't want to talk to you, I want to talk to that goddamned McKinnon. What's your name?"

"Chief McKinnon."

Her tone changed completely. "Well, I'll be," she said. "I just wanted to find out if you really did answer the phone like they say."

~

It was important to me that I stay in touch with the street-level officers in the department. I'd talk with them when they were out on patrol. I'd take the time to listen to what they had to say. Almost universally, I found that they not only wanted to make a difference, but that that was the precise reason they'd joined the force in the first place. They were my hope, and, by and large, they did the city proud.

The first precinct I visited was the 9th, which is on the far east side of the city. Smo and I surprised them when we showed up at 7:45 am for roll call. I'm sure they were shocked to see me, since this had never happened before. After roll call, I got the shift lieutenant to assign me to a patrol car. As we walked to the car, one of the officers said he'd ride in the backseat.

"No you won't," I told him. "This is *your* scout car. I'll ride in the backseat. You ride up front and answer your calls just like usual. I know this is unorthodox but I really want to find out for myself what's going on out here. It may be difficult for you to talk, but if you want to, let's do it."

At first they were quiet, but it didn't take long before they opened up. They didn't pull any punches and I appreciated that. I told them I wouldn't get involved in disputes with their supervisors—that's not my place—but anytime there was a problem with materials or policies, or something in the department needed fixing, just tell me. It was a good beginning.

While I was riding around on patrol with those officers from the 9th Precinct, my pager kept going off, as did Smo's. My office was getting calls from officers at other precincts who had already heard that we'd opened the line of communications and wanted to know if they could talk to me!

I tried to get the other command people to understand that this wasn't just something the chief should be doing—it was something they all should be doing, voluntarily. I explained to them that we'd all once been officers on patrol, but, as we moved up the ladder we tended to become removed from it. It's good to remember what it's like to go in on a robbery, to raid a dope house, or to stop someone and give them a ticket. You forget what it's like to be a street patrol officer and have people yell and swear at you, and you don't always remember how you would have responded.

My aim was to go on patrol at least once a week, but for some reason I didn't have to ride with other officers to see action. I don't know if I was blessed or cursed, but it's amazing how often Smo and I would end up making arrests. One time we caught an arsonist as he ran from the building he'd just torched. Another time we arrested a guy who was standing in the street waving a gun.

Probably the funniest incident occurred on the east side of Detroit near Van Dyke. We heard a call on the radio about a breaking and entering in progress. As we pulled up the guys took off running, so Smo and I jumped out of the car and ran after them. People on the street watched as the chief of police ran down the street after these bad guys. One by one they joined in. The next thing I knew, there was a small crowd chasing these guys with me! One guy ran right up alongside of me and said, "Hey chief, can I get your autograph?"

Needless to say, with that crowd on my side, there was no problem catching the guys. When they were handcuffed, one of them looked at the other, almost with a sense of pride, and said, "Man, the chief of police arrested me!"

As my son Jason said years later, after I had pulled a woman from a burning car on the freeway, after I had retired, "Dad, how come these things always happen to you?"

~

I worked hard to foster a good relationship with the street-level officers. I attended a meeting of the Detroit Police Officer's Association—the first chief to ever do that—and spoke to 500 union members. I made a videotape to send around to each precinct telling the officers what I expected from them and how important their involvement was to the department and to the city. I held an open forum at Cobo Hall where they could come and talk to me. I had an open door policy, so they knew they could come to my office and talk anytime they wanted to. I did what I could to revive their spirits, make them feel good about themselves and the department again, build that *esprit de corps,* and let them know that I was sincere about my desire to do a good job as chief.

I never forgot what it was like being an officer on the street. I'd been stabbed in the neck, and shot at during the riots, and I knew that it was important to remember that every day the men and women on the front line were putting themselves in that same jeopardy. I remembered Officer Schmedding, who was killed in a pawnshop robbery on Michigan Avenue. Officer Stocker who was killed when a guy shot him through a door. I thought back to Officer Glen Smith, who was shot down at 16th and Myrtle by the Black Panthers. I remembered all the officers who had gone down in the line of duty. Unfortunately, it wasn't long after becoming chief that I had to confront this again.

~

Motown Records was having a big celebration. There were countless celebrities there, as you'd expect from a record label that had more stars than a clear summer night. I was standing with my wife when none other than Berry Gordy Jr. the head of Motown, walked up to me and said, "Chief, I understand you sing." Now, understand that Berry Gordy may have produced more gold records than just about anyone in the world, and he was asking me, a guy who tried to harmonize with a street corner symphony, if I could sing. I knew that someone had put him up to it.

"Oh no, absolutely no way," I told him, laughing at the thought, but secretly thrilled that someone had tipped him off to my secret singing passion.

The celebration continued at Henry Ford's Greenfield Village. While we were there, my pager went off. The message: An officer from the 4th Precinct had been gravely wounded. I called Notification and Control, which was my contact staging group, and learned that he'd been shot in southwest Detroit and was being transported to Detroit Receiving Hospital.

"What's his condition?"

"Extremely serious."

I told the mayor, who's a deeply concerned and emotional person. He told me to keep him advised. Jose Hardrick, my driver and very close friend, and I dropped Pat off at home and headed for the hospital. I called the officer in charge of the scene and told him to make certain that when we caught the person or persons responsible nothing would happen to them. When an officer is shot, emotions run very high, and I wanted to make sure everything went by the book.

The emergency room was filled with officers. A young doctor came up to me, pulled me aside, and told me that the officer who'd been shot, had died. I can't begin to explain the emotions and feelings that I experienced at that moment. It's impossible to prepare yourself for that kind of situation.

"What about his family?" I asked a sergeant. He told me the officer had a wife and young baby. "Oh my God. Has anyone been sent to pick them up?"

They hadn't, so I dispatched a supervisor in a marked scout car to pick her up. I sent another car to pick up his mother, who lived nearby.

"Do not—I repeat—do not tell either of them that he's been killed. Just say he's been involved in a shooting. Turn your radios off. I don't want them hearing anything by accident."

The grapevine among officer's families is fast. Diane Philpot had already heard about an officer being shot and wondered if it might have been her husband Jerry. As soon as she saw the supervisor at her front door she knew it had been him, although she didn't know the gravity of the injury.

I was standing at the emergency entrance of Detroit Receiving Hospital listening to one of the accompanying cars radioing their position, getting closer and closer. I'd never had to tell a woman that her husband had died like this, and believe me, it's an unimaginable feeling.

Five minutes.

Two minutes.

As they neared the hospital, everyone started to move away from me. By the time she arrived, Jose Hardrick and I were the only ones standing there. I'll never forget the smile on her face when she got out of the car, saw that it was me, and said, "Oh, Chief McKinnon, Jerry really likes you."

I looked at her. She looked at me. All I said was, "Mrs. Philpot..." and she said, "Jerry didn't make it, did he?"

She was stunned. Absolutely stunned. I told her how sorry I was and we embraced.

"His partner, is he okay?"

I think about that a lot. There she was, having just learned that her husband had been killed and she asked me if his partner was okay. I told her he was, and she asked to see her husband. As she was being led into the hospital, Jerry Philpot's mother arrived. She saw me standing in the corridor. She saw all the officers in tears. She walked up to me, grabbed me and said, "Don't tell me my son is dead! Don't tell me my son is dead!"

I couldn't say a word. There was a look in her eyes of unimaginable pain. It was the look my mother would have had, had someone told her that I'd been shot.

"Ma'am..."

"Please don't tell me my son is dead!" She grabbed me so tight that she literally lifted me off of the ground. There was absolutely nothing I could say to ease her pain. It was the most emotional, and helpless, moment I have had in my entire career.

~

Death is sad, but it does bring people closer together. I assigned officers to stay with the family, to be on the burial detail, to be a part of the honor guard. The turnout for the funeral was overwhelming. The mayor and all of the city council attended. And, for the first time, I had to speak as the chief of police at a fallen officer's funeral. It was a difficult and emotional thing to do, but important to the officers and their families.

As a police officer, you try to separate yourself from your emotions; it's a natural reaction and something you need to do for your own preservation. But you can't let yourself become totally detached and still perform your job. I spoke to those at the funeral as a fellow officer, as a leader, and as a father. I spoke from the heart and it was absolutely gut-wrenching.

I had hoped I would never have to go through that again, but unfortunately three other officers died in the line of duty while I was chief—two of them in one incident. Sergeant Earl White and Officer Lindora Smith were in pursuit of a vehicle in the 10th Precinct when their car was struck by another police car. Both of them, along with a cadet who was riding with them, were killed. Dave Simmons called me at home, and again I found myself at Detroit Receiving and Ford Hospitals talking to the families—families that included young children. I spoke at two funerals in two days.

It was always a source of strength to me that my family was so supportive. My wife Pat stood by my side at the Philpot funeral, and I was particularly heartened by my oldest son, Jeff, who attended Lindora Smith's funeral. Several officers commented on that, telling me they were impressed that the chief's 18-year-old son felt enough a part of this extended law enforcement family to attend. He's a gem.

The last officer I lost during my tenure was Patrick Prohm, who was murdered on the east side when he pulled a man over while investigating a possible stolen vehicle. Pat got out of his car, walked over to the man's vehicle, and was immediately gunned down. The other officers returned fire and killed the man, so we never found out why he did it.

Funerals are among the toughest things for me to deal with. I'm an emotional man, as is the mayor. At Pat Prohm's funeral, we were both scheduled to talk. We were sitting together in the front pew before the service when he turned to me and said, "Ike, we're going to be strong at this funeral. We are going to be strong and we're not going to cry."

"Yes, Mr. Mayor," I said, as we shook hands and gave each other a hug.

"We're going to be strong and not cry," he repeated like a mantra, trying to drum it through his head as much as mine.

I was to speak after him, and I knew that he would set the tone—if he could be strong through it, then possibly so could I. Partway into his eulogy, he addressed Pat's three beautiful young children. "I want you all to know that you have a lot of big brothers and sisters and aunts and uncles who are here to help you." He invited the children up to the front of the church, and as he embraced them he broke down. "I want you to know we're all here for you."

The mayor was crying, I was crying, the whole church was in tears. After he finished his eulogy, he stepped back into the pew, still wiping tears from his eyes. He looked at me and said, "I've done my part. Now it's your turn."

"Thanks, Mr. Mayor. Thanks."

~

Changing an institution that's been in place for a long time isn't easy. So much is ingrained in the structure and the way it operates—both good and bad. The easy part was making sure there were good people in the key positions; changing the atmosphere was difficult. One of the things I attempted to foster was a feeling of power—not the power that comes from bossing people around, but the power that comes from being placed in a position of responsibility and then being given that responsibility. From the beginning, the mayor gave me the autonomy to run the department the way I needed to. He said so during the press conference when he announced that I'd be chief, and he meant it. This set the tone for how I would run the department: I gave the commanders autonomy to run their precincts. Of course, they had to report to me, but they knew they could work without my constantly looking over their shoulders. That was how much faith I had in the people I chose to be on my team. This helped raise the level of hope in the department and in the community, and created a feeling that things were different, that they were better, that a new age had dawned. It was a time when you didn't have to buy tickets to political functions to get promoted, a time when you weren't constantly being monitored and watched by political spies. It was a time when you didn't have to fear for your career because you got behind the "wrong" political candidate. We had a journey ahead of us, but we were off to a great start.

Early on I had the opportunity to learn that the mayor was good on his word about backing me up. He received a call one day from a young boy who said he feared for his home and family because of drug dealers in his neighborhood. The mayor asked one of his assistants to contact me so we could follow up on it. The aide forgot, but the next day the boy called the mayor back to ask why he hadn't heard from anyone. Suddenly I received a call from the assistant telling me that he blew it, and asking if I would save his butt by sending a couple of marked cars to sit in front of the boy's home to protect the family. He figured this would be a good, highly visible, public showing that would make him look good. I had to explain to him that this was a horrible idea, and no, I wouldn't do it. Just think, if anything happened to any of the drug dealers around there they'd know instantly who had called the police and the family would be in worse jeopardy than they already were. There were better ways to handle this situation. Needless to say, the assistant was none too happy about this. I explained the situation to the mayor and pointed out the potentially serious danger we could be putting the family in by doing this, and he agreed that those decisions were entirely up to me. He backed me all the way. I, in turn, backed my subordinates accordingly.

≈

Because they were too often used as weapons, the long metal Kel-lite flashlights were a source of numerous problems. Ever since they'd been used to beat Malice Green years before, the local NAACP had been pushing to get rid of them

This was Detroit's own "Rodney King" incident, though this one was fatal. In November of 1992, Malice Green, a thirty-five-year-old black man, was parked outside of a drug house at Warren and 23rd Street. Two officers, Larry Nevers and Walter Budzyn, stopped him, and a struggle ensued when they tried to get him to open his fist so they could see what he was holding. Green was struck with one of the officer's large Kel-lites and died right there on the street. Protests broke out. Mayor Young went on television and called the officers murderers. Chief of Police Stanley Knox, who was my predecessor, was sickened by what had happened and fired them. Nevers and Budzyn were convicted of second-degree murder, but their convictions were overturned. In later trials, they were each found guilty of involuntary manslaughter.

I thought about the impact that the incident had on the city and how it split the department. I thought about its effect on the officers, their families, and of course, Malice Green's family. I assigned Deputy Chief Rudy Thomas and Commander Frank Mitchell the task of finding an alternative to the metal flashlights. They found one that was nearly identical to the Kel-lite only it was made of plastic. Rudy scrounged hard and found enough money in the narcotic forfeiture funds to enable us to buy enough for the entire department, making us the first, or one of the first, police departments in the country to make the switch.

We also bought pepper spray—what most people call Mace®—for the officers. This gave them the ability to incapacitate a suspect without hitting them, and to do it from a safe distance. This resulted in an immediate and dramatic decrease in the number of prisoners that were injured, officers that were injured, and complaints against officers. I couldn't help but wonder: What if someone had done that sooner? There's no telling how many lives could have been saved.

CHAPTER *nineteen*

So many of our young people were undereducated, malnourished, had very few positive role models, and were getting into drugs, turning to crime, becoming victims of crime, and dying at an alarming rate. I knew it was critical that we do everything in our power as law enforcement officers to help them. Throughout my career, I'd seen way too many instances of young people being abused, taken advantage of, or just being neglected. I'd made it my personal goal to take every opportunity I could to talk with them, to speak with their parents or guardians, to provide a positive role model. I felt that any positive interaction I had with them would help counteract their negative feelings and thoughts, hopefully having the kind of impact Mr. Hughes and Mr. Bunche had on my life.

One night early in my career, I was called to a house near Tiger Stadium where a thirteen-year-old girl had tried to commit suicide. She was terribly despondent, explaining that she had a skin disease that kept her from going outside, lest she break out in blisters all over her body. So she spent her life inside and couldn't see any reason to live. Many were the times that I'd stop by on my rounds, or after work, so we could talk. The adult human contact did her a world of good, just knowing that someone really cared.

Although Rotation Slim may have been the cop who had the greatest impact on me, he wasn't the only one. When I was ten years old, a police officer used to come to Lincoln Elementary School and speak to us. I remember being enthralled by this friendly, nice officer, and, as chief, I wanted to put that image back in the minds of the children, replacing the negative one they may have picked up from the streets or the media.

I implemented the Chief For a Day program. I'd invite a child who had done something special—sometimes even a child I saw on the street who looked like they'd enjoy it—to come to my office and spend four or five hours with me. We'd go to meetings together and I'd introduce them as the chief. I'd take them to meet the mayor. They got an official ID card and they loved every minute of it.

One day, an officer was in the Devonshire Mall in Windsor when he saw a 10-year-old boy who looked like he'd just lost all his friends. He went over and talked to the boy, whose name was Danny Steinke. His mother said that Danny had leukemia and was going through chemotherapy. The officer came back and asked me if there was something that we could do to help him out, to cheer him up. I spoke to his parents and they brought him in to be Chief For a Day. I gave him the full works, including a helicopter ride and a jaunt with the mounted police. He loved it.

Over the next couple of months, he had to undergo forty chemotherapy treatments. I kept in touch with him and we continued to do things together. I took him to hockey games, where we sat in the mayor's box. We went to the Fox Theatre and saw David Copperfield. We went to Red Wings practice sessions and the guys on the team were great with him. Darren McCarty, Steve Yzerman, and Keith Primeau would all spend time with Danny. Through much of it, he was so sick he could hardly sit up, but he wanted to go anyway and it did him a world of good. He's in remission now, which is incredible. He came to my retirement ceremony, which thrilled me, and I choked up when he told someone "He's my hero. The chief saved my life."

Unfortunately, I wasn't always able to reach everyone like that. One day, I was at a celebration at Children's Hospital when I saw two young boys—one white, one black—and neither one was smiling. The hospital coordinator asked me if he could take their picture with me, and of course I said yes. I sat next to them, putting an arm around each one, but they wouldn't as much as crack the beginning of a smile.

I found out they both had leukemia and had gone through a great deal of physical pain and emotional suffering. I joked with them, hugged them, did everything I could to break through or get even a touch of a lopsided grin, but to no avail. Their parents tried. The hospital staff tried. The boys wouldn't even look up at me. I can't imagine how they felt, not being able to see even the slightest bit of joy or hope. I don't know if I've ever seen two sadder children. It hurt. It hurt so much.

∾

Little did I know that in my quest to reach out to the children of the city I would end up as the "Singing Chief." I began going to the elementary schools to read stories to the children. As soon as I did, the media latched onto it, and the next thing I knew a great number of schools in the city wanted me to do it. It was a lot of fun for me, as well as for the kids. One of my favorite stories to read was *Abiyoyo*, which is a great story from South Africa about a giant who comes to a village and a young boy who plays the violin to save the people. I'd get the kids singing "Abiyoyo! Abiyoyo!" and stomping their feet, which is how the people in the story got rid of Abiyoyo the giant. They loved it.

I decided to try something a little more radical, so I rounded up Jess Davis, who had retired from the department, Ernie Dernai, who worked at the Renaissance Center, and George Clarkson, who was my director of public information. We formed a singing group called the "Chief Plus Three."

There was no doubt that I was the worst singer in the group, and I was quick to admit it. My father had been a good singer. He had been a good whistler too. I can't whistle to save myself, and I can only sing respectably. At least I think it's respectable. My first partner, Jess Davis, has a wonderful voice. We'd sing as we walked the beat in the 2nd Precinct; he sang lead while I tried to harmonize. Ernie had sung in the "Shades of Blue," a group that had the number one hit, "Oh, How Happy," back in the 1960s. When I worked at the Renaissance Center, Ernie used to regale me with stories of traveling around the world singing that one hit.

So Ernie, George, and Jess could really sing. But, since I was the chief, I was the draw! Ernie sang lead on most of the songs, but we picked a few that were simple enough that I could get away with singing them. What good is it being the "Chief Plus Three" if the chief only sings backup? I would do my best and they would harmonize around me, making me look good. Hey, isn't that what friends are for?

We had our first gig singing at a school with the "Blue Pigs," a police department band that had been around for about thirty years. We alerted the media and the school was packed. I was scared to death. I have no problem with speaking to a crowd, but this was different! Holy Smokes, what had I gotten myself into?

We opened up with a Temptations song. The room was filled with people and there were cameras clicking away. I honestly couldn't have carried a tune in a shoulder holster that day. Luckily the other guys did a great job covering for me, because everyone applauded and had a good time.

This went over so well with the kids that I decided we should branch out and do something nice for the senior citizens, especially since it was right after Rosa Parks had been attacked and I wanted the other seniors to feel like they deserved the same kind of attention she had received. We organized a Senior Appreciation Day and held it at Cobo Hall. The

Department of Transportation helped bring about 3,000 people there. We solicited sponsors, who paid for hot dogs and potato chips, and for three hours we made these seniors feel special. There was entertainment, including a magician, the Blue Pigs, and, of course, the Chief Plus Three. Everyone had a wonderful time. I made sure that all of my command people were there and I had them mingle with the seniors, talk to them, make them feel special, and even serve food.

To get things rolling, I walked over to a woman, took her hand, and led her to the dance floor. She was smiling girlishly as we danced around the room. The deputy chiefs picked up on the cue and danced also. It was my version of the "Lawrence Welk Show" when all the ladies would line up to dance with the "Champagne King," except I was in a police uniform and didn't play the accordion.

The mayor stopped by and was amazed. "How did you get all these people here?"

"They came to hear me sing, of course!" I explained.

I introduced him from the stage, then dedicated the next song to him. "I know a lot of you ladies would like to dance with the mayor," I said. Then, doing my best Nat King Cole impersonation, sang the song, "Unforgettable." I thought we were going to need security the way the women swarmed around the mayor, taking turns twirling around the dance floor with him. He loved it. I loved it. Everyone had an exciting time. When it was all over, the mayor and I agreed that it needed to be done again and it became an annual affair. It was amazing. The things I had to go through to get the Chief Plus Three gigs!

~

The media loved my attempts at singing. Okay, they didn't necessarily love the singing, but they loved that I was doing it. Two TV reporters, Huel Perkins and Emery King, would razz me on the air about my singing, which only made it that much more fun. It reminded me of a story Slappy White used to tell about the great—and huge—football player Roosevelt Grier. Grier loved to sing, but the problem was that he was terrible. "*I* know he can't sing, and *you* know he can't sing," White would say. "But who's going to be the one to tell him?"

It's like the time I got to sing a song from "The Phantom of the Opera" at a fundraiser at the Opera House. The acoustics in there are incredible, making even my voice sound good. Days later, people came up to me in the market and on the street and complimented me. But what else are they going to say? "Hey chief, I saw you at the Opera House the other night and you were terrible!"?

The group continued singing. We were a part of the Christmas tape, "Blue Pig Christmas," which raised money for the Police Athletic League and later recorded a CD as "Chief McKinnon and Friends" called "What a Wonderful World." Again the listening public was very fortunate that I had a lot of good people help me out.

It was relaxing and fun. Often we rehearsed at the Renaissance Center. One time we were working on "Please, Please, Please" by James Brown, which for some reason they wanted me to sing. We were on the elevator singing because, like bathrooms, elevators usually have very good acoustics. We were in the middle of the song when the elevator stopped, the doors slid open, and standing there was a man, in awe that the chief of police was doing a James Brown imitation, singing "Please! Please! Please!" at the top of his lungs. He refused to get on the elevator, and I have to admit that I didn't blame him!

~

I've always loved going to concerts. Not surprisingly, when word got around that the chief sang, well, it meant that I got to sing with a lot of professional groups. I sang "My Girl" with the Temptations at the Fox Theatre. I sang onstage with the Beach Boys, but was so petrified that I have no recollection of what we sang. I would have loved to have harmonized with the Four Tops—or tried to anyway—but who ever heard of a Fifth Top? But there's no question that my favorite singing partner had to have been Johnny Mathis.

Mathis is easily my favorite singer of all time. Throughout the years I've purchased fifteen to twenty of his albums and have seen him just about every time he's come through Detroit. A few years ago my wife and I went to see him at the Fox Theatre along with one of my deputy chiefs and his wife. Jose Hardrick, who was my driver at the time, knew how much I love Johnny Mathis, so after the show he told me he had a special surprise and took us backstage. I stood there and up walked my idol, and he turned out to be an incredibly nice guy. We talked for about a half hour before the conversation turned to how he got interested in music: It turned out his father had been involved in Broadway shows. Mathis told me that his favorite show was Kismet, to which I replied, "You know, my favorite song comes from that play."

"What song is that?" he asked.

I started singing, *"Stand there just a moment darling let me catch my breath. I've never seen a portrait quite so lovely. How did you ever learn to look so lovely…lovely."*

Suddenly he picked up where I left off, singing, *"Moonlight, becomes you…"* and said to me with a smile, "Join me."

"…it goes with your hair. You certainly know the right thing to wear. Moonlight becomes you, I'm thrilled at the sight. And I could get so romantic tonight," we sang together.

I always knew that one day I would sing at the Fox Theatre, but I never imagined it would be with the great Johnny Mathis.

CHAPTER *twenty*

I knew that the job as chief would be a lot of work, but I never realized quite how time-consuming it would be. Twelve- to sixteen-hour days were the norm. Just about every group, organization, and block club in the city and surrounding suburbs wanted the chief to speak, and I wanted to accommodate them. It was very positive, and very much needed, but I was seeing less and less of my family. Pat did a great job of planning wonderful, quality time together—alone and with the family—which we'd manage to squeeze in somehow. But the department and the city of Detroit were the priority when it came to my time, and I started to feel the stress and tension—exactly what I swore wouldn't happen when I agreed to take the job.

There were aspects of the job that I didn't want the family to be a part of, and it was hard to shield them from it. The first hint came one morning when the phone rang at 7:00 am and a chilling voice said, "You'd better watch out for your children. I know what bus they take." Nothing strikes terror into a parent's heart more than a threat to their child. I didn't tell Pat or the kids—I didn't want them to worry—but I did order up security for the family.

Another time, Pat, Jason, and I were enjoying a performance of the Boys Choir of Harlem at the Masonic Temple when I was notified that a 911 call had come in from Jeff, our oldest son. Someone was breaking into our house!

I looked at Pat, "We're going. Now!" We hustled out of there with Jose, my bodyguard, at our side, with Pat mystified about what was going on. When we got to the car, I looked at the driver and said, "Give me the

Dr. Isaiah "Ike" McKinnon

keys. I'm driving," then told the unmarked scout car that was in front of the theater to follow us.

I hit the siren and took off. As we drove, I told Pat what was going on. To this day, she says she's never seen me drive like that, flying through the city to get home as fast as I could. When we got there, the officers had three young boys under arrest who were completely baffled about why so many police were on the scene. All they'd been doing was throwing stones at the house. Little did they know that it belonged to the chief of police.

"Who did this?" I demanded, watching them squirm.

"I didn't do nothin', man," they all said at once.

"Do you know this is my house?"

"He did it! He did it!" they said, pointing at each other.

Of course, it was innocuous, but it was a real eye-opener for me. While this wasn't a real threat, we certainly got our share of those. It's one of the big downsides to being a public person. I can handle the personal threats. After all, I'm the one who took the job as chief, but it's the threats to my family that felt blatantly unfair. After all, they were innocent bystanders. When you get anonymous calls at home filled with personal threats or comments about your family, you start to examine the reasons why you took the job. You have to stay focused on what it's all about and the good things you're doing. It really makes you start to wonder whether the safety of your family is worth it. There were times when we had to have security officers with us twenty-four hours a day and that was difficult for the family. It's not enjoyable to go to a restaurant and have an officer there at all times. It went with the territory—it just wasn't always fun territory.

It was extremely difficult for our sons to be just regular kids when, thanks to their dad being chief of police, they would sometimes have security police tagging along with them. While the potential for problems was very real, we tried not to blow it out of proportion. One time Jeff, who played basketball, tennis, and ran track, was playing an away game when a man in the stands threatened him for some unknown reason. Jeff's response was quick as he called time out and then alerted my security staff. The man looked over and saw who Jeff was talking to, and then watched as Jeff pointed him out. He took off running. It was funny as hell to see this big brave guy, who had threatened a fifteen-year-old, making a mad dash for the door.

⁓

When I became chief, I did it as a commitment to Mayor Archer and the community to effect much-needed change in the department and the city. Unfortunately, not everyone liked those changes. There were people whom I'd known for years—people I socialized with, had lunch with, and had long talks with—who didn't like what I was doing. Of course, there were those that I didn't reappoint to their plum positions because I needed to trim back the department or they were too firmly entrenched in the old way of doing things and not open to change. This was particularly difficult because I'd known some of them since my early days as a rookie, back when we were all gung ho to change the world and swore that if we got into a position of power we'd use it for good. But somewhere along the line, not all of us held onto that attitude. To them, their career came first—the city and the department were secondary. There were also those who saw my new power as chief, and our friendship, merely as a steppingstone to further their career.

It surprises me how deep some of those feelings ran. Just recently, I was waiting to play tennis with my son when there was a mix-up in the court assignment. We spoke with the attendant and the men who were playing, explaining that the court was ours to use. As Jeff and I walked away, no sooner were we out of their sight than I heard one of the men belittle me, very profanely, exclaiming how much he hated me for what I'd done to the department and how much it hurt him. It was interesting to stand out of earshot and hear that, to hear this man who was so very bitter because he hadn't been hired for a position he'd wanted. He was still upset because I hired, promoted, and fired people based on their abilities and dedication to their job, not their political patronage. To me, part of being a ranking officer meant being responsible. You came to work before the people who worked under you and you left after they did. We were paid well and I expected everyone to work for that money. During my tenure, management was held accountable for their actions. The man at the tennis courts was a prime example of someone who refused to take responsibility for what he did and how he did it. I didn't take his remarks personally: I knew that his bitterness was there long before I ever became chief.

∽

None of us in the family envisioned just how much we'd lose our privacy. Previous chiefs had been much less visible to the public.

Jeff once said that he never understood why people put the chief of police on a pedestal. When he first went to school at the University of Michigan, he would hear people whispering, "That's the chief's son," and he would think, "So what?" There's no question that people need heroes—perhaps these days more than ever. I rose up from a poor background, fought racism, worked my way up through the ranks of the police department, attained a Ph.D., and came back as chief of police. People admired the things I was trying to do and they bonded with me, and that was apparently very positive for the community.

Pat and Jeff are very private people who have never enjoyed being in the limelight. Jason, on the other hand, loves it. Pat had been warned about the loss of privacy early on by her boss, Wayne County executive Ed McNamara. He stopped her in the hall one day, shortly after the press conference announcing my appointment as chief, congratulating her on the good news. Then he asked, "How's your skin?" She wasn't sure what he was referring to, so he went on, "I've been in government for more than thirty years and I can tell you that the honeymoon with the press isn't going to last forever, so I want you to be ready. You'd better grow some thick skin."

The public eye and media attention has always bothered her more than it has bothered me. It would particularly infuriate her the way some of the press would twist the facts, report rumors, or even tell outright lies, not stopping to think about the impact that it had on people's lives. It was never aimed at me personally, but it's a problem anyone in the public eye faces.

Pat fondly remembers the day in 1998 when the last security detail person left his street post and she waved goodbye, telling our son Jason, "This is it. We're back to normal." Jason, who was fourteen, very wisely said, "Mom, it's never going to be back to normal. Our lives are changed forever."

$\sim$

Notoriety definitely has its lighter side. Twice a year there's a conference for the major chiefs of U.S. and Canadian police departments where they get together to exchange ideas and learn from each other. One year it was held in Honolulu. Since I'd only stopped there on a brief layover while in the military and Pat had never been there, we jumped at the chance to go.

It was beautiful. The temperature was perfect, the people were friendly, and the conference was productive. When the conference was over, Pat and I stayed in Hawaii for a few more days. It was especially nice because I'd been asked to speak to a group while I was there, which was quite an honor. One day we were walking along a beautiful white beach when a man walked up and said, "You're Ike McKinnon."

"Yes, I am," I said. "Where are you from?"

"Regina, Saskatchewan."

"What? How do you know who I am?"

He smiled. "We get Detroit channels 2, 4, and 7 on cable there and I see you on TV all the time. You're the chief!"

It's a very small world.

~

One thing that contributed to my public profile was that I got along well with the media. A local radio personality on an oldies station, Dick Purtan, invited me to visit his show, and it went so well that it became a regular feature. Every few weeks I'd go on the air and tell the funniest, most unusual police stories I'd witnessed or heard about. Mitch Albom, the radio talk show host and author of *Tuesdays with Morrie*, would call, as would J.P. McCarthy and Paul W. Smith.

One day I was scheduled to do a phone interview with Mitch Albom while attending one of Jason's basketball games. He went to Grosse Pointe Academy, which is well known for academics, not athletics. They were playing in Ann Arbor and were getting creamed, trailing by forty points. I called Mitch from the gym on my cell phone and we were chatting live on the air when he asked me what I was doing.

"Are you out fighting crime and keeping the city safe?"

"No," I said. "I'm at my son's basketball game."

"How are they doing?"

"Not good, Mitch. Not good at all."

The referee was standing right in front of me so I handed him the cell phone. "Mitch Albom wants to talk to you," I said. He took the phone, but continued to referee. People all over the Detroit metropolitan area listened to him chat with Mitch Albom.

Another time when Mitch called me it was about police business. It seemed that a door had popped open on an armored truck that afternoon and money had spilled out all over the freeway. A man called Mitch to say that he'd picked some up and wanted to turn it in. I told Mitch to make sure that it wasn't a setup, and then offered to get involved if he wanted me to. He got the man to agree to come to the radio station the next day with the money. Just to be safe, I had undercover officers in the lobby of the Fisher Building, where Mitch worked, and more upstairs. The man showed up carrying a box.

"Mitch. Ike. I'm glad you're here," he said, happy to see us. "Here's the money. It fell out on the freeway and I got out and picked it up. I thought about keeping it but I couldn't live with myself if I did, so here it is. I swear I didn't keep a penny of it."

I was expecting the box to contain maybe a thousand dollars. We were shocked to open it and find $110,000! Talk about an honest man.

I'm always heartened by acts like this. There was a temptation here and this man's scruples reigned supreme. And when I say I'm heartened by the act, it's only my reaction to the expression of goodness, not because I'm surprised by the act itself. I'm totally convinced of the honesty and goodness of people. I've always thought there is such a small percentage of people who are dishonest and corrupt, and that goes for people in law enforcement as well. We are a society of decent and honorable people. I hope I am never proven wrong.

$\sim$

As chief of police, I've met many famous and influential people. I've had the privilege of meeting five presidents in my life, which is five more than I ever imagined I'd meet back when I was a young boy growing up. Eisenhower was the most impressive, probably because he was my first and I was only seventeen at the time. Ike meets Ike. I liked that!

He was at Cobo Hall attending the National Auto Show and I shook his hand. It was during the 1960 election and I had a Nixon button on one arm and a Kennedy button on the other. Come to think of it, maybe I was more of a politician than I realized. I thought, "Man, I just met the President of the United States!" I never imagined that one day I'd have breakfast at the White House.

During a conference of the nation's mayors and police chiefs, Dennis Archer and I were invited to have breakfast at the White House with President Clinton. There we were, surrounded by the other mayors, the president, the vice president, and the chairman of the joint chiefs of staff, when suddenly Mayor Archer started to laugh. "Hey, homey! Look at us, two guys from Detroit having breakfast with the president. Not bad, huh?"

Not bad is right. We had fresh berries, an omelet with scallions and peppers, sweet potato hash, and pecan and phyllo crisps. I never did figure out what that last one was, but decided that I wasn't going to be the one to tell them that it wasn't any good.

I also had breakfast with the president at several National Prayer Breakfasts. A wonderful man in Detroit, Michael Timmis, and his wife Nancy invited me. I've gone three times and it's a wonderful event. Dignitaries from all over the world, of all religious groups and faiths, gather together for world peace. At one of them, I looked up and saw the president, his cabinet, members of the Supreme Court, and other members of Congress. Yasser Arafat and Yitzhak Rabin's widow were sitting next to each other at a table nearby. Strom Thurmond was there. Ken Starr, Chuck Robb, and his wife Lucy Johnson Robb (daughter of President Lyndon Johnson) sat at my table. It was incredible.

The National Prayer Breakfast was held at the same hotel where Ronald Reagan had been shot, which was where we were staying. I left my gun in my room during the prayer meeting, because naturally the Secret Service wasn't about to allow a gun in the banquet hall with the president.

After the meeting, I was waiting downstairs for a car to pick me up and take me to the airport when I realized that I was in the exact location where Reagan had been shot. The presidential motorcade was idling right in front of me. SWAT troops were patrolling the area. I turned around and saw Arafat emerge from the hotel surrounded by security people, and I was thinking, "Here I am with a gun in a holster under my jacket and no one has told me to move, checked my ID, nothing! They don't know who I am, or why I have this gun. If something bad happens now, they're going to grab me, find the gun, and I'm a dead duck!" I ran back into the hotel and waited inside just to be on the safe side.

~

President Clinton has certainly had his problems, but I'll always respect him because of the time he spent with my sons and how he was so personable with them. He was in town for a meeting at the Renaissance Center, so I brought my family along, hoping they could meet him. I was happy we had the opportunity to have our photos taken with him, but ecstatic when he struck up a conversation with Jason and Jeffrey. I stood back and thought, "Here's the President of the United States taking the time to talk with my sons!" He asked Jason if he'd ever been in a limousine, then let him sit in his. He invited my family to join the motorcade back to Selfridge Air Force Base—and of course we went along!

When we got there, Air Force One was on the runway. On the side of the plane, it read: "The United States of America." I couldn't help but think, "Damn! What's this poor boy from Detroit doing hanging out with the President of the United States?"

Everyone was lined up on the tarmac shaking hands with the president as he got ready to board the plane. The last person he shook hands with was Jason, who he embraced. "Now you take care of yourself, Jason, and continue to be a good boy," he told him. Can you imagine what it was like for an eleven-year-old boy to have the President of the United States say that to him?

Bill Clinton is a man who, I believe, truly loves his job and loves people. He's very persuasive and has a natural ability to make people like him. On another visit to Detroit, he met with the children and wives of slain officers. The man had tears in his eyes as he spoke to the children of Officers Pat Prohm, Jerry Philpot, and Lindora Smith. He listened attentively to their stories and spent time with them. When it was over, he turned to me and said, "Thank you, chief. That was very kind of you to introduce me to them." Later, when one of my best friends passed away while waiting for a heart transplant, I arranged to have his daughter, who was five, meet the president. He hugged her and spoke with her at length, genuinely concerned about her. It was a wonderful thing for him to do.

~

I met President Reagan when he was in Detroit attending a naturalization ceremony. I was pretty convinced that I wouldn't like him, but when I met him he smiled warmly and shook my hand. Suddenly I understood his attraction. "This man is everybody's grandfather," I realized. "That's why he's so comforting to so many people and makes them feel good."

My meeting with Jimmy Carter occurred after he was out of office. He appeared to be a very smart man, probably the epitome of someone who completely believes in, and understands, public service. We spent a long time talking—about fly-fishing. He told me about his favorite spots, the best lures to use at each one, and I saw that not only is the man brilliant, but completely down to earth.

Of all the presidents I have met, George Bush was the one I felt was working hard to make an impression. It's customary to have your picture taken with the president when you're at a function with him. Often these are fundraisers and people donate money to have their picture taken, but when you're a public official, you usually get a freebie. I was standing next to George Bush, waiting for the photographer to snap the picture, when he whispered loudly to an aide or Secret Service agent standing behind him, "What's his name?"

"His name is Ike," the man said.

"Ike," President Bush said with a smile, oblivious to the fact that the exchange was loud enough for me to hear, "it's so good to see you again."

~

One person I remember very fondly is Bill Cosby. He appeared at the Detroit Opera House not long after his son Ennis had been killed. He took the time to meet my family, and spoke to my sons privately for an hour. He talked about life. He talked about people. He talked about things that I'd spoken to the boys about, but I knew it meant more to them coming from him than from me. He talked about his son, and I could see the hurt, the pain, and the emotion. I watched as he spoke to my sons and couldn't help but wonder what he was seeing. Was he speaking to his son through them? He had a great heart-to-heart talk with my boys and it was a wonderful moment for us all.

Another person who was great with Jason was Elizabeth Dole. She came to Detroit when she was the president of the American Red Cross, in order to give out awards to everyday heroes. I was set to receive one because talked dow a suicidal man who was threatening to jump from the monorail of the People Mover. Before the ceremony, which was held at the Westin Hotel, Emery King from WDIV-TV introduced me to Mrs. Dole.

"It's a pleasure to meet you," I told her. "I have to tell you something. My son Jason does an incredible impression of your husband." Jason was about twelve at the time and he never failed to crack me up when he did his Bob Dole.

"I'd love to see it," she said. "Is he here?"

"No, he's at home."

"Could you call him?"

So I called Jason on the phone. "Jase, guess who I'm with?"

"Who?"

"Elizabeth Dole, Senator Bob Dole's wife."

"Uh oh. You're gonna ask me to do an impression."

"Jason, please."

He refused. Normally, he would do it at the drop of a hat, but now, when he had his big chance, he wouldn't open his mouth. She got on the phone and begged him but he wouldn't budge. Of all the times for him to turn shy!

A couple of years later, Mrs. Dole was back in town, and I met her again.

"Do you think we can get Jason to do his impression of my husband now?" she asked. I was very impressed that she remembered his name.

We tried. He still wouldn't do it. One day, maybe…

CHAPTER *twenty-one*

In late 1994, I received a call from a man who wanted to set up a meeting with me. His name was Alex Montaner, and he said the gangs in southwest Detroit wanted to sit down with each other and they asked that I mediate. "They've seen you on TV and feel they can trust you. Will you do it?"

I knew that I needed to do this. It was way too important not to. But I also knew it could be dangerous, having four warring gang leaders together in a room. Would they be able to sit together and talk peacefully? Might it be a setup to get me alone with them? There were too many variables, too many possible scenarios, and too many of them weren't good ones. I discussed it with the mayor and, of course, he was solidly behind it. I talked it over with my wife and naturally she was apprehensive. But I knew that I had to do it—this would be the first time in Detroit history anything like this had happened—so we set a date.

∼

It was a cold drive to St. Anne Catholic Church on Lafayette and St. Anne. I looked around the neighborhood, taking stock of the extraordinary security measures we'd taken. There were SWAT teams stationed around the area. Officers from the gang squad were concealed as well. And I couldn't tell who they were, but I knew each of the gangs had members scattered around the neighborhood just in case things went awry. It was edgy. There was no precedent, nothing to tell us the right way to do it other than to use our gut instincts.

Father Duggan, the priest at the church, presided. I was sitting at a table when Alex walked in leading two young men from one of the gangs. After they were seated, he went out a different door and returned with the leaders of another gang. He did this until everyone was there, each having come in their own entrance so they wouldn't mingle—or tangle—with each other. It began to resemble the conference between the Vietcong and the Americans in Paris, with each group sitting at a different corner of the table. I looked around at these young men and women who had been fighting and shooting at each other the day before, all gathered together in an uneasy meeting. So far, so good.

Father Duggan had us all join hands and we prayed. I kept one eye open, as did the gang members. The only person who had both eyes closed was Father Duggan.

I broke the ice. "So, what can I do for you?"

"You've already done something," one of them said. "You're here. I didn't think you'd come."

"Well I did, so let's talk."

And talk we did. They said they were tired of losing their friends to gang violence. They told me they wanted jobs. They told me they wanted an education. "We're tired of the killing. We're tired of living like this. But we need help to get out of it."

I was amazed. Happily amazed. They were openly and honestly asking for help so they could attain a better quality of life. They wanted the same things everyone wanted: jobs, education, and safety. I knew that if this worked, the impact on the city would be huge. There were thousands of gang members in southwest Detroit, and if I could help them I'd be helping the city in a way I could only begin to imagine. I was determined not to fail.

We talked for a long time. We started patching together a gang truce, which we finished up at subsequent weekly gatherings. Incredibly, for three days after that first meeting there was no gang violence—something that we hadn't seen in years.

We called the press and they ate it up, running front-page photos of the chief of police, a catholic priest, and gang leaders hugging. We got people in the community involved, helping any way they could. The gangs wanted jobs; representatives of Ford Motor Company and Mexican Industries opened their arms. They wanted education; we worked hard to get them back into school.

As I look back as these meetings, I think of what a historic event it was for the city of Detroit. We didn't receive the Nobel Peace Prize, we didn't receive much recognition, but the simple fact is that it did occur. It was truly amazing. I maintain, though, that if it had happened in any other large urban area in the United States we would have made the cover of

Time or *Newsweek,* but because it was the gangs of Detroit it never became a focal point for the nation. Now that I've left law enforcement, I'm not sure if these meetings have continued or not, but I just don't think there are those that are truly interested in pursuing a relationship with these youths from southwest Detroit. That is disappointing. The impact was overwhelming, impossible to measure. Today many of those gang members are happy, successful members of the community. Had that meeting not happened there's no doubt many of them would not have survived.

~

One offshoot of the meetings with the gangs was that we asked them to help us patrol the area on Devil's Night. This is an old tradition, where on the night before Halloween people play pranks like soaping up car windows, throwing toilet paper in trees, and generally being mischievous. Somehow, in Detroit it had grown into something much bigger—so big that it made the national headlines.

During the late '70s, people on the east side of the city started torching vacant buildings on Devil's Night. It wasn't long before the practice spread, and it was soon out of control. The international media flocked to town to cover the story. People from around the world would reserve rooms on the upper floors of the Westin Hotel in the Renaissance Center so they could watch the fires, trying to get up on the roof to take photographs. And it was not only dangerous, but it was a huge embarrassment and a public relations disaster. We'd gone from being the reputed "Murder Capital of the World" to "The City That Torches Itself."

To combat it, Mayor Young solicited volunteers from throughout the city to help patrol the streets, many of them municipal employees on their own time. Charlie Williams, the mayor's right-hand man, was the architect behind the program. This helped contain the fires, and instead of the hundreds they'd been having, they got it down to sixty or seventy per night.

When Dennis Archer took office, we assumed that along with our change of attitude, and those of the voters, the mindset of those who had been setting the Devil's Night fires would change too. Boy, were we wrong. As the first October approached, the mayor's executive assistant, who was assigned to coordinate the campaign, decided that he knew exactly what needed to be done—apparently not listening to those who had been around for a long time and had experience with it. There were political infighting and turf wars. He lined up volunteers, but not nearly enough. The police and the fire departments were stretched way too thin. The fires got out of control. Quickly. The mayor and I spent the night rushing from fire to fire, realizing that a terrible planning mistake had been made and that we had underestimated what was going to happen, particularly on the east side. We were crucified by the media, and rightfully so. The mayor took the heat for it, which he really didn't deserve, but that's the kind of person he is.

We were committed to not letting this happen again. The mayor appointed Glen Oliver to coordinate, and Glen started planning immediately, dividing the city into quadrants and giving police command people their own areas. We used every volunteer we could get our hands on. And we recruited the southwest gangs' help. It became a united effort between the police, the fire department, neighborhood city halls, and the community. Together we brought it under control, having fewer fires the next year than ever before. And thanks to help from the gangs, the number of fires in the southwest part of the city dropped to one. Incredible. That showed us that Devil's Night could be kept under control, and each year since the number of fires has decreased.

≈

Early in my second year as chief, I received a call from some officers who had raided an apartment building that was a drug house—the entire five-story building. It was fully outfitted with grow lights so they could grow marijuana. Tons of it. I called the mayor and told him, "You have to come see this." The television stations were there when we walked through the building, which looked like a tobacco factory, with weed everywhere in varying stages of growth, drying, and processing. By the time we left the building our clothes were coated with it. I returned to my office, while my driver took the car to get it washed. One of the guys working at the car wash sniffed a few times, looked at my driver, and said, "Hey man, you better clean that shit off you before you go back to the chief. He's gonna fire you for using that stuff."

≈

I love sports—absolutely love them. I ran track and played football, baseball, and my first love, basketball. I played with some excellent players over the years, like Alan "Jocko" Hughes, who played for the Harlem Globetrotters, and Charlie North, who went on to play for in the ABA I played with some great professionals like Dave Bing, Jimmy Walker, and Maurice McHartley. The games were part of a summer league held at St. Cecelia, a small Catholic school on the northwest side that was *the* place to be. At some point, most of the pros have played there, and I mean, these guys were good. I liked to think of myself as good too, which may or may not be the truth. You'll have to ask them.

When my sons grew older, we started gathering friends and family to play basketball on Sunday mornings. Since we went to church on Saturday evenings, we were doubly lucky—we were right with the Lord *and* had an easy time finding a free gym. This was one of the high points of my week—not just because I got to play, which I loved, but because I loved watching my boys play too. One day at the University of Detroit Mercy gym, the two boys and I were on the same team. There was a fast break. I looked over and Jeffrey was in the middle, Jason was running down one wing, and I was on the other. Jeffrey looked over and smiled. Jason looked over and smiled. There we were, the three McKinnons running a fast break together. Talk about historic events! Talk about bonding! I'd love to end this story by telling how we made the shot and won the game, but the truth is that Jeff faked a pass to Jason, tossed the ball to me, and I gave it one of my world famous hook shots and missed. But I was playing basketball with my sons, so who cares?

I've always been a runner, even as I grew older. I was twice the world champion in the over-35 men's 100- and 200-meter dashes in the Law Enforcement Olympics. I truly enjoy running and trying to stay in shape, which is why I still jog and walk regularly. One March morning I was jogging downtown, which I'd done nearly every morning for fifteen years, when I was approached by two eighteen-year-old men from Warren, Michigan who said they had a flat tire on the Chrysler Freeway. They asked if I knew where they could get a tire and rim. I told them where the nearest gas station was, but they said they were in a rush to get out of town. They offered to trade me a fully loaded shotgun if I could get them a tire and rim. I told them that I could, we high-fived, and I left after agreeing to meet at their car in a half hour. Of course, I went and called 911. The look on their faces was priceless when I arrived—in a scout car with two officers! Of course, they should have suspected that they'd picked the wrong guy in the first place, since I was wearing an FBI Academy T-shirt the entire time.

Easily, my proudest run was only a mile long—it was a part of the cross-country Olympic Torch Relay, a prelude to the 1996 Summer Olympics in Atlanta. It started in Los Angeles, and more than ten thousand people carried the Olympic torch 15,000 miles over an eighty-four-day period. Each person held it aloft for about a mile, some walking, some running, and some rolling in wheelchairs. It was a wonderful event. When they were setting it up, the mayor asked if I'd be interested since he couldn't participate—politicians weren't supposed to be involved. Of course I said yes!

It was a rainy Sunday morning, June 9th, when I ran down Woodward

Avenue to the Fox Theatre carrying the Olympic torch, the symbol of international cooperation between people. My son Jason ran next to me, along with friends Jose Hardrick and Terry McCloud, while members of the Special Response Team ran behind us carrying their flag. It was one of the more memorable moments of my life.

CHAPTER *twenty-two*

It was the last day of our annual August vacation on the Outer Banks of North Carolina when I got the call: Ten men had escaped from the Ryan Correctional Facility, a low-security state prison that sits smack in the middle of Detroit. For years people had worried about the possibility of an escape, and it had finally happened. While the state, city, and federal authorities fanned out to round up the escapees, the community was gripped with fear. With all that manpower, it didn't take long for the collaborative manhunt to capture all the escapees. I was in my office when one of my assistants told me that one of the last escapees had been apprehended and that he wanted to meet me.

"He what?"

"You gotta see this guy, chief. I'm telling you."

I went up to the fifth floor where he was being held and found a small man with a very infectious smile who reminded me of a character on "Get Smart"—Simon the Likeable. As soon as I walked in, his eyes lit up.

"Chief, how ya doin'?" he asked, offering me his hand even though it was handcuffed behind his back. I shook it. "Man, this is great meeting you. I've been watching you on TV."

"You have?"

"Yup. And you were lookin' good," he said. "You want to know what really happened with the prison break?"

Of course I did, so I pulled up a chair and sat down. "It's like this. My friend and I were sittin' around Ryan on Sunday morning smokin' weed with everyone else when we see this guy walk up on the outside and toss some wire cutters over the fence. One of the guys picked it up, cut the fence, and walked off. We didn't see any guards around, so we decided to walk, too. We just wandered around, I mean, we didn't have no place to go. We split up and I ended up at my friend's place on Outer Drive. You know, it seemed like every time we turned on the TV, there you were. Then the next thing I know, you started talkin' about a reward. Well, man, I'm sitting there with four or five people and you're saying there's like a four or five thousand dollar reward and, you know, none of these guys got no money. Ain't nobody got no money. So man, I'm suddenly scared 'cause I know one of 'em's gonna turn me in. So I figured I better get outta there."

He told me that he jumped up, grabbed his coat, and dashed outside. Just as he hit the sidewalk, a scout car pulled up in front of the house. They grabbed him and arrested him. Apparently his "buddies" hadn't wasted any time.

It turned out that he'd been to Milan, been to Standish, been to Jackson. He'd been to just about every state prison there was. He told me which ones were good and which were bad—kind of a Roger Ebert of prisons. "Listen, man. They're gonna send me to Jackson now. When I get there I'm gonna tell them guys you're not bullshitting down here. I'm gonna tell 'em 'Don't go messin' up in Detroit, 'cause that new chief, man, he's lockin' people up!'"

I looked him in the eye. "You be sure to tell them that, okay?"

"Okay, man," he said, as he shook my hand. Later that day, when they were transporting him to Jackson, I went out to watch and I swear to you, he was sitting on the bus, looking out the window, smiling and waving at me.

≈

As criminals go, he was a rarity. At about that same time, Detroit was in the grip of one of the more frightening crime waves, which for some reason the public didn't know much about—the "home invaders." They were burglars, but a very different kind of burglar. They'd hit drug houses, busting out the porch light, kicking in the door, and violently robbing the people inside. The longer it went on, the more violent they got, beating men and raping women. They were highly organized and appeared to be very well trained, so much so that I suspected that they were ex-military. These crimes were largely unreported since they were hitting houses where illegal activities were going on. We first caught wind of it from our contacts on the street. Then they hit an innocent house by mistake.

The Violent Crime Task Force went to work on it, and picked up the pattern, coming to me with what they'd uncovered. There were between eight and fifteen people involved in the home invasions, all very heavily armed. It was a very frightening situation. Once, while we had the invaders under surveillance, two of my officers watched them in action but couldn't take them down because the invaders were armed with AK-47 automatic rifles while the officers only had standard issue Glocks. They didn't stand a chance against that kind of firepower, and they made a prudent decision not to take action.

I called Joe Martinolich, the local agent in charge of the FBI, and we met with the mayor to tell him what we'd discovered. I could see the concern on Mayor Archer's face. I told him we had a plan. We knew who a couple of the invaders were. And we knew where they met. We'd keep them under surveillance until they were in their van, then follow them until they were on the freeway. Since the freeway was below ground level, it would create a natural barrier. We'd shut off traffic in both directions, trap them, and send both of our SWAT teams to take them down.

The mayor looked at me. "Ike, don't you go out there. I know you—you're planning to go."

He was right, but I promised him that I wouldn't go, and I didn't. I stayed in my office, monitoring it from there. In all honesty, this plan may have been the most difficult thing I've ever had to do because I had no doubt it would end up in a shootout, and even though my officers had flak vests, the invaders probably had armor-piercing bullets. We were as ready as we could be; we even had a tank as part of our arsenal. But these things rarely go the way you plan them. I knew that I was very likely sending at least one officer to his or her death.

The officers kept an eye on the invaders and followed them as planned. Somehow they spotted us tailing them before they even got to the freeway and got into a shootout with the surveillance officers at Livernois near Oakman. One of the invaders was killed. Two officers were wounded. We arrested them and their whole plot unraveled, luckily, with much less injury than I'd feared.

~

I've been a Detroit Red Wings hockey fan since about 1954, always hoping they'd win a championship. In June of 1997, it looked like they were actually going to do it. They were in the Stanley Cup finals and eventually defeated the Philadelphia Flyers in four straight games. The last two games were played at Joe Louis Arena, and we knew that if they won there would be a big celebration. We were prepared.

I had two seats for the game, third row from the ice. Pat and Jason watched the game while I patrolled. It became obvious that the Red Wings were going to win the game, and therefore the championship. Mayor Archer contacted me to let me know he was going down to the locker room. "Do you want to go?" he asked. Of course I did!

By the time we got there, it was jammed with people, most of them members of the press. Then the game ended and the place exploded in celebration. Atanas Ilitch, Red Wings owner Mike Ilitch's youngest son, looked at me and said, "Chief, come out on the ice with me."

I stood on the ice watching everyone in the arena celebrate. I looked around and laughed when I realized that I stood out like a sore thumb. I wasn't wearing a hockey uniform, I wasn't wearing a referee's black and white uniform, and the mayor and I were the only black people out there. Since he's light-skinned, he blends in more, so I couldn't have been more obvious.

Darren McCarty skated over and gave me a hug. So did Aaron Ward. I looked at Pat and Jason in the stands and waved at them. They were applauding and screaming like everyone else. The roar was deafening. I was waving away, trying to catch their eye. "Hey! Look at me! I'm out here with the team!"

I had to stick around afterward and keep tabs on the crowds outside, so I called Pat as soon as I figured she had made it home. "Did you guys see me?"

"Where?"

There I was, standing out about as much as a person could, and they never even saw me in all of my glory.

That night, unlike years before when the Tigers won the World Series, people were well behaved. They were celebrating, but they were doing so in a peaceful and fun way. I did have to crack down on one person, though. Many young women in the crowd were sitting on their husbands' or boyfriends' shoulders in celebration. As I walked along the area near the Spirit of Detroit statue, I noticed a young lady was perched on a man's shoulders and the guys in the crowd started the ole' New Orleans chant. Just as she was starting to lift her top, I walked up to her and said, "If you do that I'm going to tell your mother." It stopped her right in her tracks.

∽

One Friday evening later that summer, Pat and I were driving across the Belle Isle Bridge. Belle Isle is a beautiful park that sits in the middle of the Detroit River between Michigan and Canada. It's a popular spot, particularly during warm weather. We were partway across the bridge when we noticed a woman climbing over the railing getting ready to leap. I stopped the car and jumped out. I talked to her, using every bit of persuasion I could to convince her not to do it. The bridge was practically clear, but there was someone filming us. In fact, it ended up being broadcast on the news that night. While I was talking to the woman, trying to bring her back on the bridge, a guy pulled over in his car, recognized me, and started calling out, "Save her Ike! Save her!"

I called out to Pat to phone the dispatcher. The woman was still hanging on to the railing and I just kept telling her over and over, "Please don't jump, lady." I knew that if she hit the water the current would carry her all the way down river to the city of Wyandotte.

"Don't come near me," she said. I asked her if she knew who I was. She didn't.

I said to her, "I'm the chief of police and I'm asking you to please not to jump."

She looked at me and bit her lip. "Somebody raped me last night and nobody believes me. I want to die. Let me die."

"Please let me talk to you. Can I come near you?" I pleaded.

"No, I want to die."

"Let me talk with you." I was begging. "There's no reason to take your life. I can help you."

"You'll have me committed."

"No, I won't. I'm the chief of police and you have my word." She looked skeptical. "Please. Can I come to you?"

"Okay," she whispered.

I have to admit that I was shocked. I hadn't expected her to agree like that. I started to jump over the railing, slammed my knee against it, and was in excruciating pain. As soon as I got within reach, I grabbed her, not stopping to think that our combined weight might be too much for the railing and I might end up in the river with her. I managed to pull her over the railing and we both broke out in tears.

As we were sitting there on the sidewalk, with both of us crying, a dog walked by. A few seconds later, a man walked by going in the same direction.

"Thank God you saved her," the man said. "Now can you do something about getting rid of these damned stray dogs?"

～

This rescue turned out well, but as I sat in the car afterward, I couldn't help but think back to one of the rougher nights I have had in my career. The event took place right near where I just helped rescue this woman, on the banks of the Detroit River. It was a warm summer night in 1981, and the area was crowded with people picnicking, partying, and fishing. I was the field duty officer that night, which meant I was the ranking officer in charge of the department in the absence of the chief. We received a call that a van had rolled into the river with a four-year-old child inside.

When we got there, we discovered that not only hadn't the child been found, but neither had two brothers, ages seventeen and eighteen, who had gone into the river in a rescue attempt. The child's father was there and wanted to know what we were going to do. I knew that the river ran strong in that location. Very strong. I summoned the police helicopter, the harbormaster, and our dive team to the scene. Suddenly a woman walked up to me.

"Do you know where my children are?"

She was the mother of the boys who had tried to rescue the young child. I looked at her, knowing that I was about to do one of the hardest things I'd ever had to do. This was the first time in my life that I had to tell someone that their children had died. Even though they died as heroes trying to save that child, it didn't make the task any easier.

"Your sons are...they dove into the river to try and save this young child."

"Where are my boys?" she repeated.

"Ma'am, they're still down there."

"How long have they been down there?"

"I believe twenty-five or thirty minutes."

"Are they gonna be alright?"

"I don't know," I said. "I really don't know. Let's pray."

While all of this was going on, there was a group of people who had observed the entire ordeal drinking and partying. They'd been harassing my officers because they didn't dive right into the water to try and save the three young people, saying it was better to have dead cops than dead children. I tried to explain to them that we had already lost two people's lives trying to rescue the girl and that the current was treacherous, but they wouldn't hear any of it. As I tried to console the mother, some of the people in the group started throwing bottles. We ended up having to lock a couple of them up. It was a heart-wrenching night all around.

The next day at work I got a call from the Carnegie Foundation saying they were going to give a posthumous award to the two young men who gave their lives trying to save the young child. It was a wonderful gesture.

≈

Former Mayor Coleman Young, who had been ill for a number of years with emphysema, passed away on November 30, 1997. This brought a lot of deep-seated feelings out into the open, especially among people who felt that those of us in the Archer administration didn't like Young, which wasn't the truth at all. I admit to having ambivalent feelings about him. I certainly respected him as a mayor and always will, but there were things he did that I didn't agree with and thought were detrimental to the police department. But no matter what, as the chief of police and a compassionate human being, I was going to show nothing but the utmost courtesy and respect for him and his family.

There was a public viewing of his body at the Charles W. Wright Museum of African American History. Throngs of mourners showed up. Thousands of people, including me, waited in long lines out in the cold to pay their respects. The funeral was held on December 5th at a church on the west side of Detroit and it quickly turned into an event, with hundreds of people vying for a seat. Word went around that Aretha Franklin was going to sing, that celebrities like Jesse Jackson would speak, and it seemed like everyone was standing out in the freezing cold hoping to get inside.

Aretha sang a very moving song, then spoke, drawing smiles when she referred to the former mayor as "His Orneriness." It was a beautiful service in spite of the very palpable tension in the church for some of us "outsiders." When Mayor Archer got up to speak, there was a marked lack of warmth, and it wasn't just the draft from the frigid winds outside.

Family spokesperson Bob Berg said that Mayor Young's family didn't want a long procession after the service. About fifteen cars headed east down Seven Mile Raod. My car led the way. I figured that the crowds would line the sidewalks for a few blocks, but I never imagined what actually happened. People poured out of the buildings. Cars stopped in the middle of the street so that people could get out and pay their respects. People were three and four deep on the sidewalk, standing with their hands over their hearts, many saluting the former mayor. Seven Mile Road was at a standstill.

The outpouring of emotion and respect was unprecedented. Black, white, young, and old, people were crying with heads bowed. I assumed that when we got to Woodward it would thin out, but it didn't. People were two and three deep along there too, crying and waving, more than one calling out, "Take him home, chief!" as I lead the former mayor to his final resting place.

"I'm taking him, I'm taking him," I called back, and they'd give me a clenched fist power sign.

The procession was moving at a crawl. It had taken us about thirty minutes to get from the church to Woodward, which is only about three miles. As we turned south on Woodward it happened—I had to go to the bathroom. Bad. I knew that if we continued at this pace, by the time we got to the cemetery, I'd be in big trouble. As we approached a gas station near Woodward and Clairmount, I told Smo to stop, "I can't wait any longer. I've got to go to the bathroom."

The procession halted as I jumped out of the car and dashed into the gas station. I was in full dress uniform and looked very official. The people who worked there looked at me expectantly.

"Do you have a bathroom?" I asked.

The funeral procession sat at the intersection while I went to the bathroom. As I came out, I could see Smo in the car—he was just about doubled over laughing. As I trotted back to the car, people in the crowd asked, "What's up, chief? What's the problem? Something important?"

"I had to make a call, my phone's not working."

"Take him home, chief!" they said. "Take him home!"

We started moving again, slowly. The east side of Woodward was completely blocked by people who had gotten out of their cars saluting, waving, crying, and saying goodbye to Coleman Young. As we passed the library, it looked like everyone had filed out to stand on the steps. It took another forty-five minutes to get near the City-County Building, where the former mayor passed it for the final time. It was getting dark when we finally arrived at Elmwood Cemetery—the city had paid its final respects to Coleman Alexander Young. I'm sure that with his earthy manner and sense of humor he would have found my problem that day rather amusing.

CHAPTER *twenty-three*

When my third year as chief rolled around, I told Mayor Archer that I was going to retire.

"It's time to go. There are a lot of other things I want to do. Plus, I'm not spending enough time with my family, and to be honest, there's only so long I can keep up this pace."

He didn't want me to leave, but he understood.

Out of a sense of commitment to the city I loved and to the department, which meant so much to me, I stayed on as chief for another year and a half, but this was also a time of transition to the next phase of my life and career. There were other mountains to climb and other things I wanted to do with my life beyond law enforcement. The ship had been turned around and was headed in the right direction; it was time to let someone else take the helm and stay the course. I was ready to let the curtain fall on that phase of my career and use those experiences in a much broader sense. It was time to move on.

As word got out, I was approached by people from two of the casinos that were preparing to open in Detroit. They courted me well but that was not what I wanted to do. I wanted more freedom. I wanted to get back to teaching. But more than anything, I wanted to devote myself to motivational speaking.

The first time I realized that I had a talent for speaking to groups was during a speech class I took when I was working on my undergraduate degree. I was extremely uncomfortable and absolutely petrified. I waited until the last possible moment to give my talk, and when I did, I told a story I'd heard Alfred Hitchcock tell Johnny Carson on the "Tonight

Show." Partway through I noticed that my classmates seemed to be mesmerized and thought, "Wow! I've really got them!"

I got a lot of practice speaking during my tenure with the Public Information Office, but even more when I was with the Sex Crimes Unit and when Executive Deputy Chief Bannon sent me out to speak in his place. The more I did it, the more comfortable it felt. During my last year as chief I started making my public presentations more inspirational and motivational. They were so well accepted that I knew this was the way to go.

At the same time, I sat down and spoke with Sister Maureen Fay, the president of the University of Detroit Mercy, about returning to teaching. She loved the idea, and I loved the thought of being back in the world of academia. She offered me a teaching position in education and human services and I accepted.

∾

The thirteenth floor auditorium of the City-County Building was packed with familiar, smiling faces as my family and I walked in, led by Mayor Archer. Many people choked back tears, including television reporters Kevin Deitz and Cheryl Chodin, as the mayor struggled through the emotional retirement ceremony. In typical fashion, I had wanted to leave without fanfare, but Pat, who is much more perceptive about these things, urged me to consider the community and the people in the department who might want to say their goodbyes.

I introduced a number of very special people who had impacted my life. Danny Steinke, the 14-year-old leukemia survivor from Windsor, Canada. Mrs. Barton and Eddie Harris, two community activists. My sisters Bernice, Ada, and Gloria, along with my nephew Brian. My wife's family, the Sciarinis. And in an extremely proud moment, none other than Mr. Raymond G. Hughes, my mentor and teacher.

Unlike when I was appointed chief, this day wasn't a blur. Far from it. I savored every moment, smiling and speaking with friends, determined to keep it as a lasting memory. Afterward my family and a few close friends went back to my office at police headquarters for a farewell party and some final goodbyes. It was a wonderful conclusion to a long and interesting career.

∾

I spent the next few days packing up my office and preparing for the transition—mine and the new chief's. The official change of command occurred during a public ceremony held in front of police headquarters.

It was well attended. It was very emotional. It was the last time I would wear the uniform of the Detroit Police Department.

CHAPTER *twenty-four*

Ilook back on my four and a half years as chief with no regrets, but rather with a great deal of pride that during my tenure and under my leadership there was a significant turnaround in the police department and the city of Detroit. Time and again, I witnessed the forces of a city committed to change and community responsibility.

I'm proud that I made myself accessible, both to the members of the department and to the community, always working hard to make them feel included rather than excluded. In Colin Powell's book, *My American Journey,* he quotes Thomas Jefferson as saying, "There is a debt of service due from every man to his country, proportioned to the bounties which nature and fortune have measured to him." I've received so much from my country, state, and city, and have tried to give just as much back. When a young boy was struck and killed by a truck on the near west side at Dexter and Elmhurst, and a pregnant girl was shot and killed two days before Christmas for her coat, I grieved with their families. When a girl was killed by a neighbor on Christmas Eve while delivering her newspapers, and a young teen fell through the ice of the Detroit River, I reached out to the community and its members answered with prayers, gifts, and love. I encouraged members of the police department to talk, to listen, to empathize, and to console, and they responded admirably.

We instituted Operation Kid Watch, an organization that encouraged parents and neighbors to take an active role in the community by coming out of their homes and keeping an eye on children as they walked to and from school, later doing the same for senior citizens. We started sensitivity training for the officers, focusing on relations with the Hispanic and

Chaldean communities, as well as specialized training in handling domestic violence, since we knew that half of the homicides in the city involved domestic situations.

We set up a special unit to deal with the increase in street prostitution. Within a year, the number of tickets written to johns increased by 10,000 and we began confiscating their cars. Paying $700 to get them back was actually less of a penalty than having to explain it to their wives or girlfriends. In order to combat the huge increase in carjackings, we set up a special task force. To put a stop to people being robbed while using ATMs, we put machines in the precinct stations—the first police department to do so. And we set up the city's first spouse abuse unit, then mandated that if a police officer were found guilty of spouse abuse, he or she would lose their weapon—without a weapon they could no longer be an officer.

When my executive team took over, lawsuits against the department were out of control, mostly for alleged police brutality. By issuing pepper spray to the officers, we cut back significantly on these incidents, and with them, the number of officers and civilians who were injured. There were an inordinate number of false alarms being called in to the police. At one point, eight out of ten calls were false alarms. I asked the city council for an ordinance fining anyone who phoned one in. We put police in the housing projects to stop the dope dealers who had taken over, making life safer for decent people, particularly senior citizens. And we had very successful gun buyback programs.

Within the department, we discovered a number of buildings and cars that had been under long-term lease. Some of these had been in effect for so many years the department could have owned the buildings. I cancelled as many of these leases as I could. When I first became chief, 700 out of 4,000 officers were on some form of long-term disability—all being paid, of course. Some of them claimed injuries, then went to work elsewhere on the sly, while still drawing their police salary. We looked into each case and challenged those we thought were being falsified. By the time I retired, only about 200 officers were on long-term disability.

Of course, there were things I would have liked to do that didn't happen. After all, everything can't change overnight. But I have few regrets.

~

I needed to put the police department out of my mind—you just shouldn't hang around looking over people's shoulders after you leave. I couldn't dwell on the fact that I had been the chief and that I needed to make sure all of the programs I had implemented were still moving ahead. I have faith that they are. I believe they are good measures that are turning around the perception, and the reality, of the police department and of the city itself.

Detroit is my home and a source of pride for me. I anticipate wonderful things for it in the near future, but there is one fact that everyone involved has to grasp to make it a reality. There has to be a realization that not everything that needs to be done can be done within the city limits. We must bring in consultants from outside the city's borders to help shed this image of Detroit being a tough, polarized city.

In all of my years on the police force, I toiled endlessly to help alter this image, but I have come to the conclusion that the perception becomes the reality no matter what. To those of us who have lived here our entire lives, it is a terribly sad conclusion to come to. People think of Detroit as a decaying city and have it low on their list as a point of destination. They'll go elsewhere to make their fortunes. A lawmaker once told me, "The people of Detroit think of outsiders as racists who want to take over. The outsiders think of Detroiters as racist and incompetent." If these two entities don't change then the city will have some serious problems.

The city needs to be run as a business. Let's bring in the brightest and the best from around the country, or the world, and make Detroit shine as a beacon of light.

∾

I'm often asked if I'll ever go back to law enforcement, or enter politics, and my answer is an unequivocal, "No." Law enforcement was an incredible and very important part of my life, but when I stepped away from it, I took a giant step. I have realized the enormous sacrifices that my family made when I was chief, and I'm proud to say that I have made a point to spend a lot more time with my family and make up for lost time. They thank me for leaving; they thank me for leaving in good health; and they thank me for putting the family first.

In a different capacity, I'm busier now than ever before, and enjoying it more. I'm advising on law enforcement, teaching at the University of Detroit Mercy, and working on the creation of a police memorial for fallen officers in the Detroit area. I was appointed by Governor Engler to the Michigan Merit Award Board, I work with the state attorney general on the state's Mentoring Program, and I work closely with the Cornerstone Schools and Catholic Schools in Michigan. I've been hosting a series on WDIV-TV4, the NBC affiliate in Detroit, called "Stay Safe With Ike," combining my police experience with common sense to give people tips and pointers about personal safety. It has spawned a series of talks in schools about personal safety as well as an upcoming book on the subject.

But my biggest joy and focus is in motivational speaking, following in the footsteps of Colin Powell, Zig Ziglar, Tony Roberts, and Les Brown. I speak to groups large and small, church and corporate, young and old, relating my experiences in a way to help people draw inspiration and motivation, which will hopefully improve their lives. I talk about leadership, vision, teamwork, strategy, and how we can overcome obstacles and turn them into victories. If this poor child from Detroit can go from receiving charitable "goodfellow packages" at Christmas to meeting five United States presidents, Nelson Mandela, and Bishop Tutu, then anyone can rise above hardship. I tell everyone that no matter how bad things are you can always use adversity to your advantage. They should remember the things that have occurred to them and think of it as a positive, not a negative. Too many people dwell on the anger.

I remind the people I speak to that the youth of today live in constant danger. Many people don't know what that danger is like. Having received four lifesaving awards, including two as chief of police, and more than twenty meritorious citations and commendations from the department, I can tell them what it's like. I tell them so they understand what young people are up against, and how crucial it is that we reach out to help. In so many instances it appears that people don't realize what kind of impact they can make in the lives of young people. Without positive role models, children will look for their own role models in the wrong places. We really have to commit ourselves to have an impact on their renaissance. I'm so impressed by the spirit of our young people and I hope that others take the time to let it impress them.

I talk about family responsibility. It is completely necessary for men to assume their position as a part of their families. It depresses me when they do not, and I see so often how their absence has a radical effect on society as a result. It's a simple fact: Men need to recommit themselves. I talk about not disposing of our elders, instead using them as much needed mentors. I talk about the people who inspired me, hoping it will inspire others to better themselves, their family, and their community. Everybody I have met has had a positive influence on me, and I've tried to do the same in return. When I speak at corporate meetings and seminars, I discuss the importance of teamwork and management. After all, I helped turn around a very large police department; the parallels are highly appropriate.

All this is incredibly fulfilling, and I hope that others will join me as we attempt to make an impact on this life that we have been given. Stand tall.